The Language of Journalism

Second edition

The Language of Journalism

Second edition

A Multi-Genre Perspective

Angela Smith and Michael Higgins

BLOOMSBURY ACADEMIC
NEW YORK • LONDON • OXFORD • NEW DELHI • SYDNEY

BLOOMSBURY ACADEMIC
Bloomsbury Publishing Inc
1385 Broadway, New York, NY 10018, USA

BLOOMSBURY, BLOOMSBURY ACADEMIC and the Diana logo
are trademarks of Bloomsbury Publishing Plc

First published in the United States of America 2013
This edition published 2020

For legal purposes the Acknowledgements on p. vii constitute
an extension of this copyright page.

Cover design: Eleanor Rose

Library of Congress Cataloging-in-Publication Data

Names: Smith, Angela, 1969- author. | Higgins, Michael, 1967- author.
Title: The language of journalism : a multi-genre perspective /
Angela Smith and Michael Higgins.
Description: New York : Bloomsbury Academic, 2020. |
Includes bibliographical references and index.
Identifiers: LCCN 2020009105 | ISBN 9781501351686 (hardback) | ISBN 9781501351679
(paperback) | ISBN 9781501351709 (pdf) | ISBN 9781501351693 (ebook)
Subjects: LCSH: Journalism–Language.
Classification: LCC PN4771 .S55 2020 | DDC 070.4–dc23
LC record available at https://lccn.loc.gov/2020009105

ISBN: HB: 978-1-5013-5168-6
           PB: 978-1-5013-5167-9
           ePDF: 978-1-5013-5170-9
           eBook: 978-1-5013-5169-3

Typeset by Integra Software Services Pvt. Ltd.
Printed and bound in the United States of America

To find out more about our authors and books visit www.bloomsbury.com
and sign up for our newsletters.

Contents

Preface to second edition

Since the first edition of this book appeared in 2013, the world of journalism has dealt with major events, seen existent trends intensify and confronted new and unexpected challenges.

The technological changes we saw starting to take effect have been blurring some of the lines between those different genres of journalist practice that originally informed the structure of this book. Not everything has changed, of course: we still read newspapers but buy fewer and enjoy increasing access to their online versions. Moreover, we still gather round live sport on TV and radio, although we increasingly use social media to follow and comment on the action, inspired and provoked by the ongoing commentary and analysis of online news.

In response, newspapers have increased their presence on social media, with varying degrees of effectiveness. When it comes to the way we watch television in a digital environment, we see an increasing shift towards 'on demand', leading, amongst much else, to the rise of the news podcast.

This new edition of *The Language of Journalism* explores how the linguistic features of journalistic practice are influenced by all of these changes, and looks to what the evolving language of journalism tells us about our relationship with news and the truth.

Angela Smith, Sunderland
Michael Higgins, Shawlands, Glasgow
September, 2019.

Acknowledgements

We would like to thank Katie Gallof and Erin Duffy at Bloomsbury for their encouragement and support in commissioning this second edition. We also continue to be indebted to fellow members of the Ross Priory International Broadcast Talk Group, particularly Martin Montgomery, Joanna Thornborrow, Göran Erikson, Steve Clayman, Åsa Kroon, Matts Ekstrom, Kay Richardson, Andrew Tolson, Richard Fitzgerald and Marianna Patrona.

Michael wishes to offer particular thanks to his colleagues at the University of Strathclyde, and to his parents, Tam and Margaret Higgins.

Angela would like to thank her students on her Language and the Media module who, over the years, have offered their views on the first edition of this book. Colleagues in the School of Media and Communications at the University of Sunderland have also provided invaluable help, particularly Dr Alex Lockwood and Richard Berry.

The authors and publishers would like to thank the following for granting copyright permission:

Diane Courtney and Donna Roberts at Hearst Magazines Inc for permission to reproduce *Men's Health* and *Women's Health*.

Nicola Fahey and Katy Conover at Hearst Magazines Inc for permission to reproduce *Cosmopolitan*.

Laura Rowe at Immediate for permission to use the cover of *Olive*.

1

Introduction

Why should we study the language of journalism?

Journalism serves as the very oxygen of public life. Most of what we know about issues from the goings-on in neighbouring countries, to the activities of the US president, to the taxes we are likely to pay, we get from media reports. More than this, journalism extends beyond Edward Egglestone's celebrated description of 'organized gossip' to provide us with much of the raw material we draw upon to engage the world in a confident and informed manner. It is therefore not surprising that almost everyone feels able to offer normative assessments of journalistic performance, with their own instincts on what characterizes good and bad examples of the craft. However, in order that we might think about journalism in a genuinely informed and evidence-based way, comparing journalistic texts with one another, thinking about the history and practices of the profession, assessing its contemporary state, we need to have a set of tools to look at and discuss journalism in a systematic fashion. It is these tools this book hopes to provide.

Any examination of journalism is likely to be interested in *what* journalism covers. The items that make up the news agenda are not randomly assembled, nor are they the outcome of a natural and unchanging order. Rather, journalism is a matter of selection. Moreover, this is informed selection on the part of journalists themselves and the institutions for which they work. The procedures of selection draw upon particular criteria, which we will discuss later in the book as 'news values'. Knowledge on our part of these news values and their limits provides a framework for understanding why some things are thought of as having 'news' potential while most things are not. The craft of journalism is not just finding stories that meet the criteria for news, but being able to construct an account of these events that give prominence to their most newsworthy characteristics.

This leads us to the *language* of journalism. The analysis of journalism's language allows us to look at *how* journalism builds stories, how these stories function as arguments and how the linguistic construction of the story shapes the way in which it is to be understood. But the role of language is more complex than providing the component parts. Language is, after all, the most essential tool of the journalist, and it is one of the marks of the exceptional journalist that they are able to use language with creativity and style. Along with the professional practices of investigation, interviewing and fact-checking, the accomplished journalist knows that it is the ability to work with language and manipulate its emotive thrust that gives the story its shape and resonance. Without language, journalism would be no more than a picture book or a silent film. This is why it is important for us to study the language used.

To begin with, we will look at five interrelated ways in which language operates, and which emphasize its place at the centre of our understanding of journalism.

Language is social

Language is what makes us human. From our earliest months of life, we strive to communicate with the world around us through language and try to develop new skills and an expanded vocabulary in order to do this. This means that the language we acquire is one that is associated with our immediate community. As Paul Gee (1999: 82) explains, language simultaneously reflects reality ('the way things are') and constructs it to be a certain way. In this way, language is dynamic and constantly changing to reflect changing social contexts and our need to communicate within these. We expand our repertoire of linguistic styles and registers as our experiences of our social worlds increase. Accordingly, despite a considerable degree of linguistic competence, the preschool child has limited communication skills compared with those of the average university student. The language we use in the pub when talking to friends is very different from that we would use when giving a presentation in class to that same group of friends. We have sufficient linguistic competency to realize that there are different requirements placed upon us in different social contexts.

Because these competencies are rarely explicitly taught to us and yet are common conventions, we can say that we have assumptions and attitudes about language use which will reflect our attitudes about language users. This can be at a basic level of accent and dialect, where in British national TV news it is still unusual for the main news presenter to have a regional English accent that is not closely associated with Received Pronunciation (RP) (particular dispensation appears to be given to the Scots, Welsh or Irish accents of the home nations). Indeed, such is the stigma associated with certain regional accents of England, even in the twenty-first century, mainstream news broadcasters shy away from regionally identified accents, preferring the region-neutral but socially specific RP (Smith, 2009; Crystal, 2010).

The background knowledge of the reader or listener is also called upon to create a sense of common social identity, such that journalism fosters community by drawing upon a linguistic repertoire in common with the audience. The importance of this common frame of reference is never more apparent than when disputes over meaning arise, such as in the following extract from a longer interview between UK Channel 4 news presenter Krishnan Guru-Murthy and politician Godfrey Bloom on the meaning of the phrase 'bongo bongo land':

1	GB	not real;lly because (.) ah I didn't feel that I'd done anything wrong I mean I'm
2	KG	sixty-three years o:ld (.) ah that's the sort of phraseology we used years ago: (.) no
3	GB	unpleasantness (.) is at at all (.) but if [inaudible]
4	KG	[so it's just a product of being old
5	GB	[don't want me to use it (1.5) [laughs] I think it probably is (.) yes (.) ah I won't use
6	KG	it again because (.) ah I don't want to upset my party boss and my party chairman
7	GB	(.) so I shalln't use it again
8	KG	[cause Nigel Farage clearly thinks bongo bongo land is a racist phrase doesn't he
9	GB	(2) ah I think he does and again it's a generation thing 'know I'm an olde:r man
10		don't see it that way but if he says it must be so
11	KG	And you still don't understand why it is
12	GB	(3) no
13	KG	ah well I mean so that's a pretty big bone of contention I mean the thing about
14		bongo bongo land is refers to sub-Saharan Africa doesn't it
15	GB	(2.5) if you say it does
16		
17		

(from Higgins and Smith, 2017: 27).

What we see here is a clear dispute on the meaning of a phrase, with consequences for its function as an item of public discourse. The interviewer Murty maintains that 'bongo bongo land' is a prejudicial description of sub-Saharan Africa that reproduces a set of racist and colonialist attitudes to international politics. For his part, Bloom tries to argue that the term is a legitimate, if outmoded, term for corrupt and irresponsible regimes overseas, with particular aggressive military spending arrangements. From Bloom's perspective, the purpose of the term is to characterize governmental malpractice on an international stage. For Murty, 'bongo bongo land' not only lacks the clarity of meaning and legitimacy necessary for its use in news discourse, but is such a grossly offensive expression that its employment occasions a quite different news story on the attitudes and motives of the speaker.

Language enacts identity and the right to speak

The next factor that we need to understand is that language apportions a particular identity to the person writing or speaking. Often, this is unrelated to the original source of the text. Even where the person who writes a script may not be the person who delivers it, it is the one delivering the script who is responsible for it. We see this happening on a daily basis in politics, where speechwriters are often anonymous but their words can have far-reaching effects with the speaker being held accountable for what they say. John Searle (1969: 54) describes these demands as the 'felicity conditions' that we attach to utterances. Not only should something be true, but the person who is speaking should have the right to say it. This enactment of identity means we come to anticipate certain people performing certain linguistic acts, as well as being responsible for commenting on given events in their capacity as the appropriate social actor. Just as a priest is professionally entitled to declare a marriage if the appropriate conditions are met, so is a journalist entitled to express public outrage.

Through the examples to come we will find that our consideration of the appropriateness of utterances should be thought about alongside the management of personality and professional reputation amongst journalists as public figures. As Higgins (2010) has pointed out, broadcast journalism in particular includes a performative repertoire, from conveying the relative gravity of news items to animating the emotional component of an interview exchange. Accordingly, the journalists themselves are often expected to maintain a public persona in keeping with their journalistic duties, which means that a shift from one field into another, such as into campaigning or advocacy, can excite critical remark. Of course, it is also available to the interviewee to try to occupy a particular persona to their advantage, as we saw in the example above when Godfrey Bloom claims to animate the expressive lexicon of an older, and implicitly wiser and more experienced generation.

Journalistic language denotes agency and power

Just as we began by telling you that journalism is important, you can be equally assured that the vitality of journalism forms part of its very expression. In large part, this is offered as power on behalf of the readers or listeners, where language is used to imply a degree of interactivity between journalists and individual readers. Sometimes this can be through exposing wrong-doing or arguing for or against something, whereby the dynamic verb choices are often associated with leaders such as '*The Sun* says …' and 'Have your say', even 'Sign our online petition'. In this way, journalists imply there is a social influence to their profession and they pursue their responsibilities diligently.

However, the distribution of this power is hierarchical and dependent upon the needs of the story, and the opinions of certain people can be taken to be more creditable and authoritative than those of others, depending on the circumstances (Montgomery, 2007). For example, in anti-war stories, news journalism is more likely to feature the voices of mothers of service personnel who have died in Iraq or Afghanistan than the voices of anti-war campaigners who have less personal involvement in the conflict. These experiential voices carry more emotional weight for audiences and can be treated as expert opinions. Expert opinion in other contexts might come from the voices of scientists whose opinions are sought on topics such as climate change. Where the interview moves to global policies to deal with climate change, then accountability interviewees may be called in, people such as politicians and business leaders who can be held institutionally accountable for dealing with such policies. Journalism is thereby implicated in both the distribution and the exercise of power, and uses language strategically in discharging both of these.

We will find that power and identity are important components in the language of journalism. As Maxwell McCombs (2004) famously notes, journalism has the potential to influence the ways people think by setting the agendas of public discussion. News can reinforce people's beliefs about such issues as immigration, which is widely regarded in the right-wing British press as being wholly negative. It can shape opinions, such as attitudes towards political parties. Britain's best-selling red-top tabloid newspaper, *The Sun*, famously declared 'It's the Sun wot won it' after backing Tony Blair's New Labour Party prior to victory in the 1997 general election. To give a brief example of the implication of language in this, *The Sun's* style of headline writing employs non-standard English which reflects and reaches out to the working-class social identity of its perceived readers.

Language is political

As we see through all of these factors, language can be used to persuade, argue, inform and expose: it is never altogether neutral. Journalism expresses and speaks to communities of understanding, and so its language always contains layers of meaning that go beyond mere point of view. As we will see in the course of this book, journalism can only ever strive to be neutral or objective, and linguistic analysis can help to uncover the strategies and pitfalls of this endeavour. For example, we will look at how certain linguistic choices of word or phrase or grammatical structure can reveal point of view. Sometimes this is clear, such as in the reporting of the Iraq War, where initially this was referred to as the 'US *liberation* of Iraq', only for 'victory' being less than conclusive and thus that conflict came to be referred to as the 'US-led *invasion* of Iraq'. Elsewhere, news reporting of the 2008 Israeli–Palestinian conflict was articulated as Israel invading Gaza, or as Israel defending its borders. Or to take another example, the insidious demonization of young people finds stories of party-goers rearticulated as 'drunken teenagers', or more specifically in the case of women, 'ladettes', who are the subject of moral panics over a perceived decline in moral standards amongst young women.

As we suggest, language is an instrument that is shaped according to material circumstances and the purposes it is needed to serve. Language is this medium of power and can be used to legitimate inequalities and unjust social relations for political ends. It can thus be used to empower as well as disempower. Commonplace public discussion can often centre on whether a story is biased in some way, but it is through linguistic analysis that we can uncover just how this comes to be.

How to analyse language

In this book, we will be using Critical Discourse Analysis (CDA) as the main analytical model. This has developed as an area of linguistic analysis under such theorists as Kress (1985), Fairclough (1989) and Fowler et al. (1979) to explore areas of social activity and the complex relationships between language and social practice. The more dialectic view of this approach to research allows for the investigation of language as reflecting and also shaping and maintaining social realities. As developed by Fairclough, CDA is heavily influenced by Marxism and, in particular, the impact of Foucault's work on power and discourse is significant. CDA's explicitly political agenda seeks to raise awareness of the ideological frameworks that inform language choice, and the construction, representation and positioning of its subjects in discourse. This will be discussed in more detail below.

Discourse, ideology and power

The definition of discourse is open to several different views. In the area of conversation analysis, 'discourse' can be used to refer to spoken interaction. In this usage, we can 'discourse', that is, speak. In CDA, the use of discourse follows that found in cultural studies as used, but not defined, by Foucault. In this sense, discourse refers to not only language but sets of social and cultural practices. In the early development of CDA, Fairclough and Wodak (1997: 258) argued that 'discourse is socially constitutive as well as socially conditioned – it constitutes situations, objects of knowledge, and the social identities of and relationships between people and groups of people. It is constitutive both in the sense that it helps to sustain and reproduce the social status quo, and in the sense that it contributes to transforming it. This argument shows that there are important issues of power involved as a social consequence, and this in turn may have major ideological effects in that discourses 'can help produce and reproduce unequal power relations between (for instance) social classes, women and men, and ethnic/cultural majorities and minorities through the ways in which they represent things and position people' (Wodak, 1997). This definition broadly encompasses the analysis of textual form, structure and organization from the level of phonology to generic structure. Within linguistics, different approaches have tended to focus on specific levels. For example, in French discourse analysis, the focus is on lexical semantics, whilst in critical linguistics the focus is on grammar and lexis. However, as Riesigl and Wodak point out:

> Whether analysts with a critical approach prefer to focus on microlinguistic features, macrolinguistic features, textual, discursive or contextual features, whether their angle is primarily philosophical, sociological or historical – in most studies there is reference to Hallidayan systemic functional grammar.
>
> (2001: 8)

Texts function within 'discourses'. We should think about discourses within the Foucauldian tradition, they are historically constituted bodies of knowledge and practices that shape people, giving positions of power to some but not to others.

Ideology

The level of debate on the precise meanings of ideology is a reflection of its continuing importance in academic thought, particularly as it pertains to the relationship between media and the social environment. Marx and

Engel's celebrated definition in *The German Ideology* positions ideology as 'the ideas of the ruling class' that are lent their dominance through might, but are subject to change to meet the developing interests of whichever ruling elite prevails. For this part, Louis Althusser (1971) directs us to the role of such 'ideological state apparatuses' as 'the media' in sustaining a particular set of ideologies, and suggests that a dominant ideology positions us as 'subjects' of the governing system, and is integrated into the practices of daily life (we will see more of this idea of lived practice when we come to look at nationalism later).

For the purposes of this book, we shall be taking ideology to mean a 'set of beliefs or values that can be explained through the (non-cognitive) interest or position of some social group' (Elster, 1982: 123). In this way ideology is structured discourse, and is directly or indirectly based on or generated by a set of mutually interdependent categories. As adopted by Eagleton and Macdonald, this approach to ideology does not deny how ideology operates through 'such devices as unification, spurious identification, deception, self-deception, universalisation and rationalisation' (Eagleton, 1991: 222).

Antonio Gramsci's notion of hegemony is useful to theorize how ideology works in winning support for particular ways of seeing the world. Gramsci (1971) claimed that dominant groups rule by consent rather than force, and obliged to combine leadership, compromise and judgement in order to cultivate sufficient support for their continued rule. The tactics involved in retaining a 'hegemonic bloc' of support will include attempts to harness a 'national-popular' consent and a claim to represent an organic and indisputable 'common sense'. However, ideology is only ever encountered in what Bennett (1998) refers to as a 'compromised form': one which is not static but forever shifting through the constant negotiation and contestation of differing and shifting social and political circumstances. Gramsci (1971) notes that the political breakdown of an 'organic crisis' where the previous common sense is rendered disputable lays the conditions for an alternative ideological settlement to emerge. A nuanced approach to ideology therefore acknowledges the agency of social subjects to make, albeit limited, choices depending on their cultural positioning instead of being reduced to being merely the effects and vehicles of power.

Texts and social structures

Texts can be very useful in assisting in developing an understanding of how discourses, ideology and power operate in society. As Fairclough has commented, they can be seen as 'sensitive barometers of social processes, movement and diversity, and textual analysis can provide particularly good indicators of social change' (in Jaworski and Coupland, 1999: 204). They provide evidence of these ongoing processes, and thus offer a rich source of data for research. In this book, we draw on a variety of media texts which include print, broadcast and digital platforms. A much-criticized aspect of Foucault's hugely influential work on discourse is that he failed to provide specific and detailed evidence of texts to support his historical studies of discourse. In spite of this, the specifically linguistic analysis of texts provides support to Foucault's underlying genealogical methodology for analysis. Jürgen Habermas (1987: 259) claims that 'language is also a medium of domination and social force. It serves to legitimise relations of organised power. In so far as the legitimations of power relations, [...] are not articulated, [...] language is also ideological'. This is a claim that would probably be endorsed by most critical discourse analysts. Commenting on the usefulness of textual analysis in this area, Fairclough remarks:

> [It] is increasingly through texts [...] that social control and social domination are exercised (and indeed negotiated and resisted). Textual analysis, as a part of critical discourse analysis, can therefore be an important political resource.
>
> (in Jaworski and Coupland, 1999: 205)

As Wodak (2002) explains, a fully 'critical' account of discourse requires a theorization and description of both the social processes and structures which leads to the production of a text, and of the social structures and processes within which individuals or groups as social historical subjects create meanings in their interaction with texts. Consequently, three concepts feature in CDA: the concept of power, the concept of history and the concept of ideology. If we accept that discourse is structured by dominance, then the history of a given discourse is tied up with the history and development of those systems of dominance. In other words, it is situated in time and space, and the dominant structures are legitimated by ideologies of powerful groups. CDA makes it possible to analyse pressures from above and possibilities of resistance to unequal power relationships that are made to appear as societal conventions. According to this view, dominant structures stabilize conventions and naturalize them. Explicitly, the effects of power and ideology in the production of meaning are obscured and acquire stable and natural forms: they are taken as 'given'. Resistance is then seen as the breaking of conventions, of stable discursive practices in what Fairclough (1993) refers to as acts of 'creativity'.

To the extent that much of social science shares a concern with the relationship between text, practice and relations of dominance, CDA provides a generally useful resource. As we will see throughout this book, different journalistic products produce 'common sense' discourses such as the examples briefly discussed above (such as Israel 'invading Gaza' or 'defending its borders').

The development of CDA

Critical Discourse Analysis grew out of the work of British and Australian pioneers of Critical Linguistics, particularly Fowler and Kress, in convergence with the approaches of British discourse analyst Norman Fairclough and the Dutch text linguist Teun van Dijk. CDA has produced the majority of the research into media discourse during the 1980s and 1990s, and 'has arguably become the standard framework for studying media texts within European linguistics and discourse studies' (Bell and Garrett, 1998: 6).

In the tradition of critical theory, CDA aims to make transparent the discursive aspects of societal disparities and inequalities. CDA in the majority of cases takes the part of the underprivileged and tries to expose the linguistic means used by the privileged to stabilize or even to intensify inequalities in society. Most frequently, CDA has an explicit socio-political agenda, a concern to discover and testify to unequal relations of power which underlie ways of using language in a society, and in particular to reveal the role of discourse in reproducing or challenging socio-political dominance. It also offers the potential for applying theoretically sophisticated frameworks to important issues, so is regarded as being a particularly useful tool for researchers who wish to make their investigation socially active. Work in Australia in the 1990s, initially in the field of educational linguistics, has led to what Martin terms 'Positive Discourse Analysis' (Martin and Wodak, 2003: 4) 'to characterise ideologically orientated research and intervention that examines positive developments with which to make the world a "better" place, and draws on these to intervene in related sites – as a mode of inquiry complementing CDA's focus on language in the service of abusive power' (Martin and Wodak, 2003). This continuity of explicit political intent underpins the approach's ongoing concern with a theory–practice dialectic. One of the strengths of CDA is that it bases concerns with power and ideology in the detailed linguistic analysis of texts.

Helmer (1993) makes the argument that storytelling too can operate ideologically by 'creating and sustaining symbolic oppositions that enable members to position themselves and others in the organisation', and as such narrative 'serves to strategy the organisation along lines of power, authority, gender and ethics' (1993: 34). In relation to gender, Helmer makes the point that women are forced to 'play the patriarchal game' in order to gain some form of economic and political advantage when they are disadvantaged both politically and economically. So, for example, a female actor may turn up at a 'red carpet' event in a revealing outfit, knowing that this will attract media attention. At the UK premier of the 2009 film, *Nine*, Nicole Kidman's short shirt in an otherwise demure outfit attracted a great deal of media comment, whilst her co-star Daniel Day-Lewis's extravagantly high-waisted striped trousers and embroidered shirt passed without comment (e.g. *Daily Mail*, 4 December 2009). The British former glamour model, Katie Price, attempted to reclaim public sympathy after a messy divorce by claiming sexual abuse by her former husband. In Price's case, this plea for sympathy was only partially successful as more dominant stories of her drunken nights out appeared alongside media stories which mused on the whereabouts of her young children. In both cases, discourses that prioritize a conservative performance of femininity are drawn upon to criticize the women concerned.

The model that Fairclough developed for CDA is useful for researchers who share his concerns with language, discourse and power in society. Fairclough's (1995) model has three components:

1. The first dimension is *text or discourse*, which includes micro texts (e.g. vocabulary, syntax) and macro levels of text structure, as well as interpersonal elements in a text.
2. The second is analysis of *discourse practices*. This looks at how a text is constructed and interpreted, and also how it is distributed. Analysis of discourse also considers the discourse practices of different social domains (such as political discourse). Fairclough calls these 'orders of discourse'.
3. The third dimension is analysis of *social practices*, focusing in particular on the relation of discourse to power and ideology.

More simply, this is a method of situating language in its social context (Fairclough's first and third dimensions), looking at the producer–consumer interaction (the second dimension). This is something we will come back to repeatedly in the course of the subsequent chapters. For example, we will see how magazine language can be best understood by exploring the social world it is produced in, and for whom in this world it is directed. So we will use CDA to explore how a women's magazine produced in the twenty-first century has concerns with the #MeToo movement, and is underpinned by commercial factors that are widespread in contemporary Western society.

One criticism of CDA has been that the definition of a text is so narrowly defined in that it would not reveal the wider social and discursive practices to be found in other objects for study. However, as Fairclough acknowledges, the wide-ranging cultural studies definition of text 'can obscure important distinctions between different types of cultural artefact, and make the concept of a text rather nebulous by extending it too far' (1995a: 4). Nevertheless, as Fairclough goes on to say and to explore in more detail in his subsequent work, the broader definition of text is useful in contemporary society as 'texts whose primary semiotic form is language increasingly [have] combined language with other semiotic forms' (1995a: 6). Yet even this has a number of dimensions of meaning. Written texts can be multisemiotic, for example, in the typographical design and inclusion of graphics. The co-presence of other semiotic forms within a primarily linguistic artefact interacts to produce multisemiotic texts.

What emerges is a multifunctional idea that texts can be viewed as social spaces in which two fundamental social processes occur at the same time. This involves the analysis of 'the cognition and representation of the world, and social interaction' (Fairclough, 1995a: 6). As Fairclough points out:

> Texts in their ideational functioning constitute systems of knowledge and belief (including what Foucault refers to as 'objects'), and in their interpersonal functioning they constitute social subjects [...] and social relations between (categories of) subjects.
>
> (1995a: 6)

So this view of texts helps to bring about a practical demonstration of Foucault's (1981) claim about the socially constitutive properties of discourse and text.

Media texts can be categorized under several different genres. As Fairclough had argued, a 'genre' may be characterized as the conventionalized, more or less schematically fixed use of language associated with a particular activity, as a 'socially ratified way of using language in connection with a particular type of social activity' (Fairclough, 1995b: 14). However, Threadgold observes that genres can be more flexible, unpredictable and heterogeneous (Threadgold, 1989). For example, Montgomery et al. (2019) show how the interpretation of openly available social media posts by public figures is contingent upon the norms of the particular platform and the assumed addressees. So the genre of 'Twitter banter' produces a certain form of expressive latitude, and enables the production of statements that would be offensive and indictable in any other context.

Foucault's (1970) concept of 'orders of discourse' differs in its use by different CDA practitioners. It is taken by Fairclough to 'refer to the ordered set of discursive practices associated with a particular social domain or institution [...] and boundaries and relationships between them' (1995a: 12). In general terms, orders of discourse are the ways in which power relationships are enacted, where one participant is in a more powerful position than the other. The more powerful participant evokes this hierarchy of power through language choices, for example, through choosing to accept or reject a contribution or through evoking certain discourses. This is what happened in the case of the 'Twitter banter' mentioned above, where Tweets that may be thought of as appropriate to a 'contrarian' journalist – in this case Toby Young – enter into a different regime of institutional judgement when the writer moves into government service, and thereby becomes accountable to that overarching discursive order. The boundaries of such discourses are not clearly defined in many cases, and are constantly shifting, reflecting orders of discourse as mediation between the linguistic and the social. Fairclough (1995) regards changes in the order of social discourse as being in themselves part of wider processes of sociocultural change. Official, expert knowledge serves as a means of building up structures of 'truth' or 'normalisation', regulating what can be said and what can't be. Such debates more recently include those surrounding climate change, where the voices of those who oppose policies to limit climate change (such as reducing logging in the Brazilian rain forests) have been largely removed from the debate as presented by the media. Instead, we hear the voices of scientists who live thousands of miles away from the rain forests, but whose contribution is prioritized. Populations can be carefully controlled through the associated disciplinary structures, where certain discursive practices are legitimized and others (usually those of the least powerful) are delegitimized. As Threadgold puts it, such 'expert knowledges thus discursively produce the objects of which they speak and simultaneously exclude those categories which cannot be accounted for within the established "truth"' (1997: 137). As we will see in the more detailed studies that follow in this book, the differently positioned writers and readers across a range of texts that have been produced drawing on differing knowledges and discursive practices will allow for an exploration of aspects of identity and culture.

Drawing on Foucault's earlier work on discourse, Fairclough argues for the place of CDA, suggesting that it

> ought in contemporary circumstances to focus its attention upon discourse within the history of the present – changing discursive practices as part of wider processes of social and cultural change – because constant and often dramatic change affecting many domains of social life is a

fundamental characteristic of contemporary social experience, because
these changes are often constituted to a significant degree by and through
changes in discursive practices, and because no proper understanding of
contemporary discursive practices is possible that does not attend to that
matrix of change.

(1995a: 19)

Orders of discourse are thus viewed as domains of hegemony and hegemonic
struggle. This may be within institutions such as education as well as within
the wider social formation. In this process, the ideological investments of
particular discursive practices may change.

Many of the journalistic texts we will look at are spoken, some of which
are interactions between two or more participants. This means reference to
conversational analysis will be relevant to our exploration of language. John
B Thompson (1995) and Martin Montgomery (2007) have explored how
spoken interaction can operate in the media. There has been a lot of research
in the field of conversation analysis (Hutchby, 2006), and many of the features
of such naturally occurring talk are relevant to our study of how language
operates in the media. For example, if we accept that the basic expectation of a
question is that it requires an answer, then we anticipate there being more than
one participant. This links with the principle of turn-taking in conversation,
which is one of the basic rules Sacks (1992) listed as components of such
interaction. Other features include that in turn-taking where one person talks
simultaneously with another, then this is for only a brief time: one participant
will 'yield the conversational floor'. We will explore how this relates to broadcast
media texts in more detail later in this book.

Linked to conversation analysis is Fairclough's work on conversationalization
and synthetic personalization (1989). This can be found in various forms of
public sphere texts in the late twentieth century that are relevant to our study
of media texts. This, as we will see, is closely aligned with informal, spoken
language and could be said to be part of the tabloidization of the media (Smith
2009). In Fairclough's definition of synthetic personalization (2001), a media
text's producer – whether it is spoken or written – uses linguistic strategies that
attempt to present a personal dialogue between individuals. This is achieved

through drawing on strategies such as employing personal pronouns (e.g. 'Tell *us* what *you* think'), dialectal features that are presumed to be used by the intended audience/consumer of the text, for example, '12 *hacks* to feel amazing' appearing in a heading for mindfulness ideas in a health magazine aimed at women and drawing on supposed common knowledge. Grammatically, the use of the question format implies a direct interaction between text producer and reader/listener. For example, the commonly used advertising slogan 'Have you got yours yet?' anticipates the prospective consumer will respond and rush out to acquire the advertised goods or service.

As Wodak (2002a: 11) comments, an important perspective in CDA is that it is very rare for a text to be the work of any one person. In texts, discursive differences are negotiated; they are governed by differences in power which are themselves in part encoded in and determined by discourse and by genre. Texts are often sites of struggle, showing traces of differing discourses and ideologies contending with the dominant power. It is not only the notion of struggles for power and control, but also the intertextuality and recontextualization of competing discourses that can be revealed by CDA.

The three-dimensional framework for CDA as outlined by Fairclough includes the analysis of discursive practices. This relates to the processes of a text's production, distribution and consumption, and ensures that a text is not isolated from the institutional and discoursal practices within which it is embedded. Within the scope of our analysis of media texts, the text can be reviewed with reference to the diverse ways in which it could be interpreted and responded to. This approach to text analysis owes much to Morley's work on audience reception in media studies (1980), extending this from examining the moment of reception to consideration of how texts are taken up and transformed in various spheres of life (such as the family, work and leisure activities).

In this model of CDA, the Gramscian theory of hegemony (in analysis of sociocultural practice) is combined with the Bakhtinian theory of genre (in analysis of discourse practice – defining genre as discourses, narratives, registers, etc.). Bakhtin's work on text and genre (in Jaworski and Coupland, 1999) argues for the inclusion of intertextual analysis as a necessary complement to linguistic analysis in the studying of texts, as such an approach draws attention to the dependence of text on society and history in the form of the resources made available within the order of discourse. According to Bakhtin (1986: 65), genres 'are the drive belts from the history of society to the history of language'. This dynamic conception of intertextual analysis highlights how texts can transform social and historical resources, and how genres can be mixed within a text.

Intertextuality

The term 'intertextuality' was devised by Kristeva in relation to Bakhtin's discussion of the transposition of sign systems of carnival, courtly poetry and scholastic discourse into the novel (Threadgold 1997: 66). Her use of this term closely follows that of Foucault, although Foucault himself did not use this label, instead describing how statements can only exist in connection with other statements (1981: 98). At its most fundamental level, as Bakhtin observes, intertextuality is inherent in language as part of its comprehensibility. The speaker

> is not, after all, the first speaker, the one who disturbs the eternal silence of the universe. And he [*sic*] presupposes not only the existence of the language system he is using, but also the existence of preceding utterances – his own and others' – with which his given utterance enters into one kind of relation or another (builds on them, polemicizes with them, or simply presumes that they are already known to the listener).
>
> (1986: 124)

Bakhtin's writings on text and genre (1986) argue for intertextual analysis as a necessary component of linguistic analysis, an argument that has been taken up by Kress and Threadgold (1988), Thibault (1991), Talbot (1995) and Fairclough (1992, 1995a, 2003). The use of the concept of intertextuality in linguistics has been particularly important in relation to the development of CDA. In this model, as Threadgold states, 'texts are now understood to be constructed chunk by chunk, intertextually, not word by word, and there can thus be no link between text and context except through the intertextual resources of this discursively produced subjectivity' (1997: 3).

Fairclough expands on this, arguing that intertextuality is used to draw attention to the dependence of texts upon societal and historical discursive formations in the form of the resources made available within the order of discourse (Fairclough, 1995a: 188). The concept of cultural capital, as explored by Bourdieu (1991), is relevant here as access to the range of texts from which interpretation may be drawn is not equally distributed. We saw this in a more oblique way in the Murthy-Bloom interview above, where the interviewee claimed to lack particular aspects of contemporary cultural capital, as a way of asserting an expressive clumsiness. Culler (1981) and Barthes (1970/1975) expand intertextuality to include the reader as a constituent component. Culler described intertextuality as the general discursive space in which meaning is made possible and intelligible (1981: 103). Thus, for Fairclough:

> Discourses and texts which occur within them have histories, they belong to historical series, and the interpretation of intertextual context is a matter of deciding which series a text belongs to, and therefore what can be taken as common ground for participants, or presupposed. [...] Discourse participants may arrive at roughly the same interpretation or different ones, and the interpretation of the more powerful participant may be imposed upon others.
>
> (1989: 152)

So the intertextual resources each person has available to them can be limited, leading to a restricted understanding. This link between intertextuality and power makes it an important part of Fairclough's three-part model for CDA. As he argues, 'intertextual analysis crucially mediates the connection between language and social context, and facilitates more satisfactory bridging of the gap between texts and contexts' in his three-part model, whereby intertextual analysis occupies a mediating position (1995a: 198).

Holquist relates Bakhtin's notion of the dialogic nature of intertextuality to power, arguing that 'a word, discourse, language or culture undergoes "dialogization" when it becomes relativized, de-privileged, aware of competing definitions for the same things. Undialogized language is authoritative or absolute' (1981: 427). As Holquist suggests, there is a difference in the degree to which texts may be 'dialogic'. Fairclough (2003: 47) offers a general summary of the effects of the dialogicality:

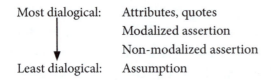

Most dialogical: Attributes, quotes

                          Modalized assertion

                          Non-modalized assertion

Least dialogical: Assumption

In this way, we can understand this model as 'less dialogicality' carrying with it consensus, with a 'normalisation and acceptance of differences of power which brackets or suppresses differences in meaning and norms' (Fairclough, 2003: 42).

In a manner that increases with access to social media and blogging platforms, the study of journalism produces evidence of individuals using officially produced and sanctioned and other forms of information for their own means. As Foucault says of the power to watch and judge:

> One doesn't here have a power which is in the hands of one person who can exercise it alone and totally over the others. It's a machine in which everyone is caught, those who exercise power just as much as those over whom it is exercised.
>
> (Foucault, 1980: 156)

In a manner that transfers readily to the discursive powers of journalism, Foucault's conception of power sees it dispersed rather than contained to a few, even if unequally. Although Foucault (1983: 217) expresses an anxiety to distinguish 'power relations' as a whole from 'relationships of communication', it is worth emphasizing that shifts in the production of journalism have democratized the very apparatus of expression. Such that the discourse of journalism is the exercise of power, it can therefore be as much about resistance as reporting. Yet this appearance of resistance is something Abu-Lughod has argued that we ought not to romanticize, arguing rather that 'we should learn to read in various local and everyday resistance the existence of a range of specific strategies and structures of power' (1990: 53). In identifying and exploring the manifestations of 'resistance', we can see in greater detail the complex workings of power relations.

The use of dialogical elements in a text allows for other 'voices' to be heard, and is at its most dialogicalized in this development of intertextualization. This can be analysed in terms of power relations: whose 'voice' is allowed by the text's producer, what are they allowed to contribute, how is this being contextualized? This 'editing' process of dialogicalization can be used to exclude as well as include other voices. We will look at this in detail in the chapter exploring magazine features.

Where we go from here: the structure of the book

Having explained some key components and techniques of language and discourse analysis, the rest of the chapters are divided according to genre and media platform. This spread of media platforms is designed to enable us to look across a diverse range of journalistic forms, and to examine both written and spoken forms of news delivery. We have set out the book so that different chapters develop particular themes, and draw upon varying strategies of analysis. In doing this, we are able to explore how the several angles of analysis we have called upon tease out different discourses. Some of these discourses we will find across more than one chapter, such as the place of gender across both magazines and newspapers and the importance of national identity in both broadcast news and sports journalism. Others, such as sociability in broadcasting, are concentrated within particular chapters. Importantly, this should not be taken to mean that these discourses are contained within given genres. Quite the opposite in fact, as you are invited to think about and explore how various discourses, communicative strategies and forms of commonality might have a role across various forms of journalism. In using this book, you might productively reflect on the place of gender in broadcast news, for example, as well as perhaps whatever strains of national identification sustain through online journalism. We are therefore dedicated to showing you some sense of the diversity not just in the language of journalism and the contexts in which it appears, but in the dynamism and flexibility in how it has come to be used, and the tools that are available to examine it afresh.

Broadcast journalism

We begin by looking at broadcast journalism. As we will see, the dialogic aspects of journalism are found in interaction between participants who are using spoken language. The features of spoken language we find here have become increasingly informal, something Fairclough refers to as 'conversationalisation' of public discourse (see also Smith, 2009). The general features of such spoken language that we will look at in this chapter have fed into printed forms of journalism, as we will see in later chapters. In this chapter, we will explore a variety of journalistic texts from the broadcast media, including television and radio. In addition to scripted news, the chapter will examine the interaction between news journalists and studio-based news presenters, and interviews with non-media interactants. The relevance of visual aspects of TV broadcast journalism will also be discussed, including the multimodal elements of the live online news broadcasts. Much of the analysis will be informed by issues of balance and bias in individual journalists' broadcast reports, and the implications of liveness and unscripted journalism. The chapter will also examine how language study offers an insight into the processes involved in turning reporters' notes into a broadcast script.

Magazine journalism

After looking at spoken language used in broadcast journalism, we move to the simulation of this in print media. We will find that Fairclough's work on synthetic personalization can be applied to written texts where the strategies of spoken language will be applied in the creation of a friendly, approachable community of readers. This chapter, therefore, will explore the linguistic features and discourses of magazine journalism. It will look at the visual components of magazine cover design, and the influence of advertising on the forms of visual and writing used in magazines. The chapter will also look across the various genres of magazine, including literary and celebrity magazines, and will examine the implications of these for journalistic writing with particular reference to issues of gender.

Newspaper journalism

We will now move on to the language found in newspaper journalism, seeing how the features of spoken language we have seen in previous chapters are most often found in news headlines. As well as differences between 'quality' and 'popular' newspapers, and those between national cultures, the various genres of newspaper journalism – editorial, opinion, news and feature coverage – will be outlined, and the significance of the linguistic styles employed in each one fully explored.

Sports reporting

In this chapter, we will explore how this variety of journalism is a combination of spoken and written language. In looking at sports reporting, we will focus on the characteristics of sports commentary. Of particular interest to this chapter will be the extent to which sports commentary draws upon and deals with the norms and expectations of other forms of journalism, such as the distinctions between description and comment. The chapter will also be concerned with the management of spontaneity and the consequences of live broadcasting for journalistic form, and the recreation of this in print media and the expansion of this into online media such as Twitter and media outlet-specific live reporting blogs. We will also draw on the way national identity comes into sports reporting, and particularly how this can be used to articulate prejudices that are akin to racism in certain high-profile contexts.

Digital journalism

The final chapter will draw together elements found in other chapters that relate to more recent developments in journalism. It will look at the online presence of newspapers and broadcasters, examining both the formative constraints and the development of new forms of journalistic language. The chapter will show how multi-modal approaches to discourse are useful in comprehending the relationship between language and other aspects of online provision, and will look at the influence of these emergent forms on institutional news sites as well as other social media platforms such as Facebook, Twitter and YouTube. We will see how the conversational nature of journalistic language is present in this form, in particular as untrained reporters – citizen journalists – increasingly make an important contribution to media reporting. It will look at the development of a 'structured unconventionality' within amateur and fan journalism, and will reflect upon how this has flourished in the online environment. The chapter will also examine the linguistic characteristics associated with news-dedicated weblogs, taking account of such factors as the emphasis on opinion and authorship, and conclusions will be offered regarding the implications of these for journalism practice. The chapter will examine the extent to which the practices of citizen-produced journalism are becoming incorporated within conventional journalism institutions, both online and elsewhere. We also expand this chapter to link back to our first chapter on Broadcast News, where journalists tackle reporting through podcasts.

News values

This introductory chapter will conclude with an introductory summary of news values and their importance. Before we can pursue any insight into the language of journalism, it is necessary for us to have a system for reflecting upon what it is journalists are trying to do. In a now well-known essay on Norwegian news coverage of international affairs, Johan Galtung and Mari Ruge (1965) proposed a series of 'news values'. Their taxonomy is driven by the observation that the great majority of events in the world are not thought of as 'news'. Even occurrences of some import will be deemed newsworthy in some contexts and not in others. One instance of town hall corruption will dominate local headlines, while meriting just a passing reference in the next jurisdiction; whereas a more lurid example of local political malpractice, or one with a link to a national figure, will be admitted to the wider news agenda. Their initial list of twelve is as follows:

1. **Frequency** determines that the optimum news event should unfold at a rate appropriate to the given media, be that an hourly radio update or a weekly newspaper.
2. Events are judged according to a **threshold of magnitude**, the larger, or the more violent, the more newsworthy it is.

3. News should be **unambiguous**, militating against events that demand a complex or nuanced interpretation.
4. An event should be **culturally meaningful**, to the extent that it should have a particular resonance with the journalists and audience in their lived environments.
5. The event should be **consonant** with what the news organization expects to cover.
6. Yet, news should have an **unexpected** element of novelty and surprise.
7. Also, news is often a **continuation** of an ongoing story, as much as once an event becomes a part of the news agenda, further developments on the same story are likely to be covered as well.
8. Further, an event also has to fit with the **compositional requirements** of the news outlet at a given time, where particular genres of story have to be catered for, including politics and sport for example.
9. In addition, references to so-called **elite nations** are of more consequence than places considered more economically and culturally removed.
10. Likewise, **elite people** such as political leaders and celebrities are more important in determining news selection than others.
11. On the other hand, **human interest** enjoys considerable prominence in news, including a tendency to emotionally empathize with the subjects of a story where possible.
12. Finally, the imperative for **negativity** guides journalists towards unanticipated disasters and scandal, rather than the routine and functional.

Together, these news values constitute the 'common sense' behind what makes a compelling news story: on some occasions offering an explicit framework for judging one potential story against the next, while more often describing an unconscious set of professional perceptual practices.

There have been several reconfigurations of Galtung and Ruge's original taxonomy. Allan Bell (1991: 156–9), for example, introduces four additional factors.

1. The first of these is that news is defined by **recency**, meaning that journalism routinely places stress on the timeliness of the account.

2. Also of importance is the **competitiveness** between new producers, seeking to outperform one another in the breaking of news stories, the depth of detail and sometimes the production of spoilers.
3. In addition, Bell emphasizes the influence of **attribution**; that is, the quality of sources available and whether these correspond with such values of elite persons and human interest will help in determining news selection.
4. Linked to ideas of professional quality is the fourth consideration of **facticity**: the obligation of news to truthfulness, and the availability of vivid and visually striking evidence to foreground claims to truth; including the expressability of this facticity using what Harcup and O'Neill (2017: 1482) refer to as 'arresting … audio visuals'.

Another of the most notable revisions of news values is that by Tony Harcup and Deirdre O'Neill (2001, 2017), who introduce the considerations of cultural and technological change to the list. They direct towards the following recent developments:

1. An increase in the newsworthiness of **celebrities**, as part of a broader emphasis on gossip and updates relating to the entertainment industry, often engaging a symbiotic relationship across journalism and other media genres.
2. They also call our attention to the **political agenda** and **market position** of the news organization itself, linked to the notions of ideology and industry competitiveness described above.
3. Lastly, the importance of the purchase of a story across social media platforms in terms of its **shareability.** The shareability of a news story is sometimes colloquially referred to a 'clickability', or 'clickbait'. One of the features of such stories can be the enticing bullet-pointed list, or 'listicle'. Such lists are often promoted through numbers, such as 'Top 15 places to stay in Sweden', or 'Premier League: 10 things to look out for this weekend'.

On the basis of even this short discussion, it is useful to note that lists of news values are always subject to emphases and the predominant and technological cultures of production and consumption. By way of illustration, a number of complementary taxonomies are available – Teun van Dijk (1983) offers a slight variation, for example. However, for conceptual clarity, it is useful to settle on a defined list, and be ready to discuss its utility as well as its limitations. This is a list of the ones we have chosen to highlight:

- Frequency
- Threshold
- Unambiguousness
- Cultural meaningfulness
- Consonance
- Unexpectedness
- Continuation
- Composition
- Elite nations
- Elite people
- Human interest
- Negativity

(Galtung and Ruge, 1965)

- Recency
- Competition
- Attribution
- Facticity

(Bell, 1991)

- Celebrity
- Entertainment
- The agenda of the news organization
- Shareability

(Harcup and O'Neill, 2017)

As we progress through this book, then, the use of CDA as outlined above will help us explore how journalistic language articulates these news values in the various genres and modes by which 'news' is spread by the media.

2

Broadcast journalism

Introduction

This chapter will now explore some of the methods and principles described in the last chapter within the fields of broadcast journalism, including examples from both radio and television. Broadcast journalism offers up a peculiar set of practices and opportunities for thinking about the relationship between language and journalism. This should come as no surprise, since as journalism moves across different media platforms it develops to take advantage of whatever innovative forms of engagement become possible. As we noted in the introductory chapter, one of the characteristics of both scripted and unscripted broadcast talk is an increase in informality (Montgomery 2007; Smith 2009). In spite of the pronounced asymmetry in power in the status of the journalist against the listener or viewer, and even as the content of the news aspires to accuracy and the projection of authority, broadcast journalism increasingly tries to style itself as unstuffy and relaxed.

As we read on, we should keep in mind that journalism is primarily concerned in the production of news content to agreed professional standards, both informal and codified. Throughout the chapter, we are also therefore going to look at those issues of balance and diligent practice around which the professional quality of broadcast journalism is judged. We will look at how news values are emphasized in the news script as it is broadcast, and reflect on how attention to the conventions of news, both recent and emerging, helps us understand the way language is used in broadcast journalism. However, we will also stress the complexities and opportunities that the increasing multi-modality of broadcast news offers to the analyst.

Broadcast and interaction

The imperative of informality in broadcasting manifests itself in what appears to be a loosening of the relationship between the broadcaster and the audience. The capacity for engaging in 'para-social interaction' – described by Horton and Wohl (1982: 188) as 'the illusion of face-to-face relationship [between the audience and] the performer' – has become a valued skill amongst broadcast journalists. And as media platforms begin to converge, with digital and online communication streams allowing varying degrees of live audience feedback, what Paddy Scannell (1996) describes as a conversational mode designed to place the audience at their ease edges more towards a genuine two-way arrangement. Increasingly, news producers are able to interact with the audience in real time, involving members of the audience through phone-ins, text messaging, Twitter and emails. This is an arrangement capable of intervening and altering the content of the journalism as the broadcast proceeds, in addition to generating ongoing conversation and comment and sustaining feedback afterwards.

Because media organizations are rarely required to pay for this extra audience-generated content, it is relatively cheap to produce. In her 2003 book *Ordinary Television*, Frances Bonner notes that one of the characteristics of such 'ordinary' television is the inclusion of 'direct address of the audience, the incorporation of ordinary people into the programme and the mundanity of its concerns' (Bonner, 2003: 3). Göran Eriksson has explored the steady increase in the numbers of 'ordinary' participants since the 1990s in the Swedish context (Eriksson et al. 2017). Joanna Thornborrow (2015: 5) has argued that, in a digital age, 'the distinction between ordinary people and media professionals is no longer a sufficient or an adequate one in terms of describing the variety of identities and range of performances we find' on our screens. However, this blurring of the ordinary and the professional is something we can see as being a shift towards the ordinary, as is particularly found in the genres of broadcasting traditionally regarded as the domain of public participation: docu-soaps, makeover shows, talent shows, game shows, commonly glossed as 'reality TV'. We can easily begin to imagine how this quest for the everyday voice is manifest in such genres as 'reality television', but what we will also find is that this drive to draw upon the sympathetic qualities of the 'ordinary' is to be found in the structure of many news stories.

News values, balance and bias

Notions of balance and the avoidance of bias are central to the way we think about 'good' journalism. The Platonic realization of these ideals is notoriously elusive, and Michael Schudson's (2001) discussion of 'objectivity' sees it as a professional ideal rather than an inflexible template for everyday practice. Journalists are normally content to offer as balanced and truthful an account of events as possible, in a manner that will engage the audience. Yet, agreed professional standards are central to much broadcast presentation, as they are across journalism more generally. This is most formalized where there is a 'public service' arrangement, such as in Britain. There, codes of conduct demand impartiality and fairness of terrestrial television news. British broadcast regulator Ofcom specifies that news be characterized by 'due accuracy and presented with due impartiality' (Ofcom, 2017: 28), requiring journalists not only to vouch for the veracity of their story, but to acknowledge appropriate alternative viewpoints in its interpretation.

But there are other expectations placed upon broadcast news that can be applied more broadly. In both the introduction and the newspaper chapter, we have spoken about the various sets of news values that journalists apply in determining what should count as news, and deciding where the emphasis should be placed in the composition of the news text (Galtung and Ruge, 1965; Bell, 1991; Harcup and O'Neill, 2017). In his book on broadcast news, Martin Montgomery (2007: 4–9) presents a version of those news values, configured to accord with the needs of the broadcast conventions and its technological affordances. Here is a selection, along with some explanation of why they are particularly pertinent to broadcasting:

Recency/timeliness

The first is an increased emphasis on recency. As the plural of 'new', news has timeliness at its core. The development of twenty-four-hour rolling news coverage has had a major impact on the way news is reported (Cushion and Lewis, 2010), with a stress on emerging information. As Montgomery points out, time has developed as an explicit part of interpretation in news broadcasts, with such phrasings as 'Today's top stories' and 'Coming up in the next hour' essential for emphasizing the freshness of the product and holding the attention of the audience. As we will see later, this imperative towards more frequent updates is also reflected in the expression of certain forms of contingency.

Conflict

Conflict is also a frequently used criterion for selecting news, the emotive potential of which carries particular weight in the performative context of broadcast news delivery. Conflict itself can range across rowdy sports events, neighbourly disputes and political wrangles, as much as it does international warfare. In additional to its emotional appeal, the newsworthiness of conflict stems from an impetus towards negative rather than positive news (Harcup and O'Neill, 2017), as well as the disposition of news to draw upon the empathetic potential of images of extremity and personal suffering (Chouliaraki, 2012). On another level, conflict allows the imposition of binary oppositions, such as 'us' and 'them', West and East, right and wrong, freedom and tyranny (Hodge and Kress, 1993: 162). Such reports carry with them visual images that need to be clear and iconic, often enabling the use of overt stereotypes.

Proximity/cultural relevance

As we will see from the examples given below, in the same way as newspapers (Higgins, 2004), broadcast news is obliged to stress recognizable cultural relevance, including a lower-threshold for domestic matters and culturally familiar regions and nations, that with its own broadcast reach. Certainly, broadcasters defining themselves in terms of their global outlook, such as BBC World, Al Jazeera, Russia Today or CNN, are more likely to carry stories from outside of their own national setting. But, as Montgomery (2007) points out, there remains an emphasis on cultural proximity, such that countries with a perceived 'commonality' with the news provider or with localized implications are given precedence.

Balance and bias in times of conflict

It is obvious that there are a number of underlying values that motivate broadcast and other forms of journalism, and we have looked at just a few of these. We are now going to look at the work journalism does to maintain normative principles of journalistic balance, looking at the contentious area of international conflict. A study commissioned by the United Nations and World Bank emphasizes media and journalism's role as agents as much as reporters of international conflict, and recommends a heightened media sensitivity to glocalized sensibilities and the often subjectifying and exclusionary character of international coverage (Betz, 2018). Added to these informal responsibilities are the cultural and regulatory constraints on how journalists can report such potentially fraught areas as violence and war.

However, Justin Lewis and his colleagues highlight the tensions between the professional ethos of the journalist and this culture of expressive restraint, quoting British journalists' reflections on how they dealt with the 2003 Iraq War, censoring their reports to accommodate the sensibilities of UK terrestrial television:

> Many of our interviewees felt that British television news coverage was too sanitised and would have liked to have shown more, whilst mindful of the need of protect children from the effects of such coverage [...] Guy Kerr (C4's managing editor) believed that British viewers will become increasingly suspicious of mainstream British news if it continues to be sanitised.
>
> (Lewis et al., ud: 14)

We will examine this further with reference to a report by the BBC's former chief news correspondent, Kate Adie, on the American bombings of the Libyan capital, Tripoli, in April 1986. Briefly, the background is one of heightened tensions between the US and the Libyan governments, which had led to journalists being despatched to Tripoli in the weeks leading up to the attack. The technology available in 1986 meant that Adie's reports were largely pre-recorded down unreliable telephone lines between Tripoli and London, or else filmed and sent back to London by air freight. There was little opportunity for interrogation of her reports at that time, but this journalist was severely criticized by the Thatcher government in Britain and the Reagan government in the United States for alleged bias towards Libya.

In particular, one report she recorded for BBC News shortly after the American bombing of Tripoli came in for extensive criticism (Higgins and Smith, 2011), but is interesting for its strategic focus on civilian casualties. Adie's report (Table 2.1) begins with a subtle but clear indication that she is subject to reporting constraints: namely this is a 'guided tour' (line 1) rather than independent excursion. The orchestrated nature of this tour is further highlighted by her metaphor-laden description of the farmer as 'holding up his trophies for our benefit' (lines 2–3). However, she is also careful to draw attention to the wayward nature of the American bombing, using a shared lexicon of distance and direction: the farm is 'one mile north of the military base' (lines 8–9).

Table 2.1 Kate Adie, *BBC1 Nine O'clock News*, 17 April 1986.

A guided tour of the orange groves south of Tripoli:- the remnants of	1
Tuesday's raid, marked with the sign Texas Instruments. The farmer holding	2
up his trophies for our benefit, found in his chicken run through the oranges	3
and the olive trees a line of bomb craters. The Libyans have buried their	4
dead, and are dealing with the aftermath of the raid: there's still shock – but	5
much of the tension has gone – the official line is that they do not want war	6
with America. There are still many reminders, though. Including several	7
missiles and a variety of fragments and debris. Another farm – one mile	8
<u>north</u> of the military base – also boasting craters and crumpled metal. But as	9
we were looking at this, two small boys were being curious in a street near	10
the French Embassy in Tripoli; they brought a red object out of the rubble –	11
and took it to a young man nearby. He was shown to us on the operating	12
table. It's difficult to know if he's a victim of the American raid or of the huge	13
amount of ordnance directed by the Libyans at the aircraft.	14

The journalist's accompanying notebooks indicate that she reconfigured her report to take into account a new story that arose as the journalists were travelling back to Tripoli from the farm where they had been taken, the sudden emergence of which is indicated on line 9 by the contrastive coordinating conjunction 'but as we were looking at this', which situates her viewpoint amidst a community of journalists engaged in collaborative activities of surveillance. The journalist's management of the process from notebook to broadcast script shows the creative work undertaken to encourage empathy with the local civilians, with the initial 'two small boys were playing' altered to 'were being curious' (line 10). Such a reformulation adds a more human element, using a mental process verb to accord a positive and shared human quality in place of an, albeit sympathetic, physical activity.

In keeping with the findings of Lewis and colleagues, work was also undertaken by the journalist to minimize explicit descriptions of injuries and their cause. Background documentation also tells us that Adie and several other journalists were taken to the hospital where the injured man was being treated: the broadcast is accompanied by shots of the backs of the surgeons working in the operating theatre. As to the cause of the man's injuries, a gap is left in the coherence of the report between the retrieval of the 'red object' (line 11) and his presence in the operating theatre. In terms outlined by Dan Sperber and Deirdre Wilson (1995), the absence of explicit details here leaves the viewer to apply the criteria of presumptive 'relevance' to the shift in circumstances, moving from the implicit threat of the bombsite to the scene in the operating theatre. Crucially, such formulations also comply with an internalized obligation to avoid explicit reference to 'gory details'.

The composition of this extract also tells us a great deal about the procedures of truth-telling. It is clear from Adie's notebooks that she was uncertain as to the origin of the explosive device that caused this injury. Whilst the Americans had stated they had only bombed 'military targets', it was also established the Libyan armed forces were unlikely to have the specific device that was the cause of this injury. In the report, this is reflected in the strategic hedging 'it's difficult to know' (line 13), which combines the acknowledgement of the limited corroborated evidence with a personal point of view, here explicitly referenced to Adie's own processes of comprehension. While it has the appearance of a spontaneous expression of indecision, Adie's notebooks show this last sentence was the subject of extensive rewriting and careful consideration. For all the care and contingency involved in the process of composition, the final description is emphatic. In the final broadcast script, the bomb raids on line 13 explicitly remain ascribed to the active agency of the Americans, while the possibility that the device might have originated from 'the huge amount of ordnance' (line 14) used by the Libyans is ameliorated by their use of such weapons in defence.

Although military conflict is an unfortunately common resource for journalism, we can see how strong political views can also be reported in a manner that mobilizes the dynamic of confrontation and conflict. In the UK, there is a statutory broadcast obligation in public service broadcasters (the BBC, and to a lesser extent ITV and Channel 4 News) to provide 'due partiality and due accuracy and [to avoid] undue prominence of views and opinions' (Ofcom, 2017: section 5, p. 1). If we look briefly at one report from Channel 4 News, we can see how the reporter, Ciaran Jenkins, is attempting to bring balance to a report following US President Trump's attacks on non-white politicians in that country. Jenkins's report is framed by a live-to-studio contextualization (Table 2.2):

Table 2.2 Channel 4 News, 30 July 2019.

CJ	The attacks keep coming (.) therefore so does the backlash (.) Donald Trump was in Jamestown Virginia today at a (.) milestone celebrating a milestone in American democracy (.) that was boycotted by black Democratic (.) politicians (.) Donald Trump's speech was then interrupted by another local politician (.) who held up signs including one that read (.) deport hate (.) so two (.) overarching questions really (.) does Donald Trump really want this row (.) a row that is being defined by racism and does it help him (.) we've been to Macomb County that's not far from here (.) a place that voted for Obama and then for Trump (.) a place that Donald Trump knows is key to his hopes of re-election	To camera live from Detroit	1
		Footage of Trump standing at podium with protestor holding up posters	5
			10
			15

On lines 8–10, Jenkins sets out the matter his recorded report is going to explore, phrased as an 'overarching question' as to the possibly strategic nature of Trump's attacks. While presented as an informed summary, its claim to facticity underpinned by the adverb 'really', this frames the story as one on the priorities and prospects of Trump rather than the content of the accusations against the president.

The report then proceeds with brief questions to members of the public in a vox pop arrangement, preparing for what is going to form the longer, five-minutes pre-recorded package. As noted above, the nature of the attacks Trump had made was based on race, and this core controversy is reflected in the composition of a vox pop segment drawing equally between black and white voters. Within the individual piece, this manner of composition projects an immediate claim to balance, with the sets of interviewees animating alternative perspectives. In the following extract (Table 2.3), Rod is a black male and Laurie is a white female:

Table 2.3 Channel 4 News, 30 July 2019.

CJ	Do you believe that he is using racially inflammatory language	1
	deliberately to grow his base?	2
Rod	Yes (.) absolutely	3
CJ	Do you think it can work [shot of Trump 2020 cap]	4
Rod	It has	5
CJ	Is there any way he could be even more racist [shot of white	6
	couple] that would make you stop and take pause and make you	7
	think (.) right I can't support this guy any more?	8
Laurie	I don't know (.) I'd have to wait and see what lines he crosses	9

Jenkins's initial question on lines 1–2 includes an implication that racist language was indeed used, but the question is framed as an inquiry as to whether this use is part of a deliberate strategy on Trump's part. Interviewee Rod produces a succinct affirmation to both questions and their underlying assumptions on Trump's intentions. The question to Laurie also contains an underlying assumption that the tweets were racist (Jenkins asks if Trump could be *more* racist, which carries the implicature that he is racist already). However, the question this time is not about whether this is deliberate, but whether Laurie could continue to support Trump. Outwardly, Laurie's answer is more ambiguous, but includes a contrary implication that there is a 'line' that Trump has not yet crossed. In this way, the report is set up as a disagreement between the two interpretations of Trump's attitudes and prospects, setting the terms of the subsequent discussion between the various racial groups.

Jenkins's full report reverses the structure of the preview, with the Trump-supporting couple interviewed first (Table 2.4). When Laurie initially claims to have not been paying much attention to the most recent events relating to Trump's attacks on the non-white congresswomen, he asks:

Table 2.4 Channel 4 News, 29 July 2019.

CJ	Is it a deal-breaker for you if the president does something that's (.)	1
	racist (.) says some racist things.	2
Laurie	No because a lot of people are thinking it (.) should he saying it (.) no	3
	(.) because he's in that higher power and he's supposed to be setting	4
	an example	5
CJ	[vo diner kitchen] Laurie voted for Barak Obama (.) so did Macomb	6
	County as a whole (.) twice (.) before embracing Donald Trump (.)	7
	she's proof the Democrats' hope (.) that his most extreme rhetoric	8
	would alienate suburbia (.) may be misplaced	9
Laurie	[Laurie and Robert at diner table] It's it's not so much about what's	10
	on the news as how (.) our little world is going (.) right now our little	11
	world is going well	12
Rob	[close-up of Robert's Trump 2020 hat] It's gonna come down to the	13
	people (.) who's who's feeling it and who's not and I see a lot of	14
	those shops getting filled back up (.) people money	15

Jenkins's question on line 1 reformulates the previous question, without the implicature that Trump has been racist, here it is tentatively 'if' he does something racist. This allows Laurie the opportunity to express the view that anything Trump says is okay, as it is just giving voice to the disempowered. A brief pause then occasions a change of footing in which the interviewee asserts the unacceptability of those in power saying 'racist things' (lines 3–4). This is then followed by a voice-over where the journalist Jenkins frames the ambiguity in Laurie's response as indicative of a deeper contradiction on voter intention, towards which the report's commitment to truth inevitably propels it ('she is proof' of a flawed plan, line 8). This point is underlined with the final two utterances from Laurie and Robert, asserting a broader political complacency amongst the beneficiaries of the current arrangement. That camera shot of Robert's Trump 2020 campaign hat at once undermines the neutrality of this interpretation while producing a synecdoche for the broader Trump support.

The report then shifts to the group of black interviewees (Table 2.5). This produces apparent agreement with Laurie's point that Trump is just saying what others are thinking, but in this case, the interviewees direct the report towards the interpretation of these views as racist and unacceptable:

Table 2.5 Channel 4 News, 29 July 2019.

Tomicka	It speaks to what they've always thought about people of colour and	1
	now you have someone in the highest office in the land telling that it's	2
	okay that you feel like that because I do too	3
Joel	Donald Trump is a symptom (.) the disease is the racism that has been	4
	in this country since the time it started (.) what he's saying is what a	5
	lot of people want to hear	6

While the preceding section portrayed some ambiguity, both of these con-tributions enter into a more empathically socio-historical frame, situating Trump's words within an interpretation of US history. Both interviewees as-serting Trump as the animator of a longer-standing set of prejudices ('someone in the highest office in the land telling', line 2, 'Donald Trump is a symptom … what he's saying', lines 4–5); Tomicka claiming the normalizing of racism, Joel's stressing a broader historical context.

The final part of the interview (Table 2.6) features the voices of the black interviewees, framed by Jenkins's questions and voice-over.

Table 2.6 Channel 4 News, 29 July 2019.

CJ	He says he's not a racist and his supporters say he's not a racist so	1
	when you read a tweet that says something like (.) those	2
	congresswomen should go back [shot of Jackie shaking her head] to	3
	their own countries crowd sh-shouting (.) send her back (.) can you	4
	remember what that felt like	5
Jackie	Yeah	6
CJ	To you	7
Jackie	I can remember (.) I have been told go back to Africa [.] and like I	8
	told them (.) I didn't come here voluntarily (.) but if you're brown	9
	(laughing] or if you have any melanin in your complexion he talks	10
	about you he started off with the Hispanics he went on to Mexican (.)	11
	he called them rapists and murderers and after he went to the	12
	women (.) he has degraded women (.) after that he has gone to the	13
	blacks and he will continue this tirade that he has with degrading	14
	people until we have a revolutionary war and that where I think we're	15
	headed	16
CJ	[voice over] We're headed towards the contest Donald Trump may	17
	well have been spoiling for (.) two sides entrenched opposing visions	18
	for America's soul (.)	19
Rodney	Even though both of them may feel patriotic (.) the patriotism has	20
	to do with love your country (.) loving your country is above all	21
	racism [cut to US flags fluttering in the breeze] We need everybody	22
	to make America great because America was great before Donald	23
	Trump came into office (.) and there's a guaranteed fact the United	24
	States is going to be great long after Donald Trump has gone.	25

In order, again, to demonstrate balance, the journalist Jenkins's question on lines 1–2 is formulated as a challenge to the assumption that Trump is racist, by drawing on wider voices, including those of the earlier white interviewees. In terms of how this is anchored on screen, however, the accompanying visual images are of the black interviewees shaking their heads in disagreement. Seeking elaboration, the question is turned directly to Jackie, enjoining her to share her personal experience as a black woman. This is produced using a prompt ('To you') that foregrounds Jackie's implicit claim that has also been told to 'go back to where you came from', which she confirms on line 8. That she has a prepared response to this speaks of a lifetime of subjection to this abuse. The report then allows Jackie the floor to extend this experience to the various groups said to have suffered discrimination from Trump. Her utterance finishes with the violent metaphor of the end point to this disharmony being 'revolutionary war'. Importantly in terms of the overall tenor of the report, rather than disputing this with Jackie, we find Jenkins in voice-over supporting the view that there is a strategic use of racial division, although this is ameliorated in by the hedging of 'may well' (line 18).

With a visual cut to US flags fluttering in the breeze, the report finishes with the words of one of black interviewees, Rodney, who reinforces the view that racism is less important than patriotism. In terms of its political implications, the segment foregrounds a concern for the wider national picture than the small-world view of the white interviewees. Thus this report seeks to bring out both views in the argument about racism in the US political context, but through a mixture of ordering (who gets to speak and when) and visual elements, as well as offering the space for emotionally vivid elaborations, the pro-Trump side of the argument is given less credence than the words of the black voters, who are the ones who are given the final call to unity in this report.

A number of scholars have remarked on the antagonistic component of contemporary political culture (Mouffe, 2005; Higgins and Smith, 2017), and on the prevalence of emotionality in giving weight to political perspectives (Wahl Jorgensen, 2019). From this brief analysis, we can gather some idea of the problems a journalist faces when reporting a variety of expressions of a story, and how these can be dealt with using careful expression. Constrained by the censorship imposed by the Libyans in the case of Adie's report, with Adie not free to report what she wants from where she wants. This is linked to a desire not to upset the host government and thus risk expulsion from the conflict zone. At the same time, the reporter has to be aware of their audience and, in the case of war, the conventional expectation of a clear 'us and them' distinction (Hodge and Kress, 1993: 163). It was clear that the American bombing raid had largely missed its military target and had instead caused civilian casualties, the journalists' dilemma here was one of how to express the news in the context where the side we would ordinarily align ourselves with – the cultural centre of the news text and all its values and assumptions – may be culpable. In the case of the Channel 4 report by Ciaran Jenkins, whilst there is no military conflict, there is a political battle between the Left and Right. In this latter case, the report contains voices from both sides, but the framing and sequencing allows one view to carry more weight. We will see shortly how the 'second place' voice (in the case of the Jenkins interview, the black voters) has privilege.

Broadcasting and sociability

It is clear, therefore, that broadcast journalism has to apply news values while, to some extent, balancing and feeding the cultural expectations of the presumed audience; and doing these things while at the same time discharging duties of impartiality. However, at beginning of the chapter we presented the drive of broadcasting to be present itself as sociable. We saw traces of this in the section above, when phrasings such as 'two little boys' emphasized the emotive qualities of the story, in a manner designed to appeal to the sympathies of the viewer. In this section, we are going to take this a stage further and look how many features broadcast journalism has in common with informal talk. It will therefore be useful for us to look at some of the main features of conversation analysis, and reflect upon how these can help us to understand broadcast talk.

Where journalists either address the camera or speak into a radio mike, they engage the audience as though they were addressing them directly, whether that is as a collective or as individuals (Scannell, 1996: 24). We have already noted that the technique of appearing to address the audience directly is referred to by Horton and Wohl (1982) as 'para-social interaction'. While the 'para-social' version differs from ordinary interaction in that it is addressed towards physically absent others, it nevertheless proceeds as though it were subject to the normal responsibilities of face-to-face interaction: not least, to be seen to make an effort to be understood to appear conscious of the feelings and pleasures of the addressee.

What this demands is the cultivation of a means of performing the journalistic function of delivering the news while calling upon the linguistic mechanisms of interaction. This short extract from the BBC Radio 4 *Today* programme (broadcast 31 August 2012) shows an example of this as the presenter Evan Davis hands over to a special correspondent, Adam Brimelow, who will present the next item in the show (see Table 2.7):

Table 2.7

Davis	It turns out it's never to late to turn to a healthy lifestyle (.) this is	1
	according to a huge new Swedish study of two thousand older people (.)	2
	healthy living (.) adds years (.) to life expectancy in fact five or six	3
	years (.) Adam Brimelow is BBC health correspondent and can explain	4
	all (.) Adam (.) the five or six ears (.) was that just what you got from	5
	being healthy (.) when you were old or was that what you got when	6
	you were being healthy over your whole life	7
		8
Brimelow	Yes the unusual thing about this study is it focuses specifically on	9
	people (.) who lived a long time already (.) people over seventy five	10
	[report continues]	11

The extent to which co-presenters are used as a conduit for the enactment of informality is notable. What is apparent is therefore an easy mix of conventional face-to-face interaction with the co-presenter, which it is assumed that the audience will overhear, where Davis addresses Brimelow as 'Adam' (line 5), and para-social interaction with the audience, where 'Adam Brimelow' is introduced to listeners as 'BBC health correspondent' (line 4).

This relative informality on the part of the broadcaster can also set in place a particular relationship between the audience and the news. In short, the journalist aligns themselves with the audience in occupying the position of someone 'trying to make sense of' the news, and always looking to establish what the immediate impact of the news might be on 'ordinary people' such as the journalist and those in the audience. Brunsdon and Morley (1978: 87) describe this position as that of the popularizing journalist, who uses the language of the ordinary person against the obscuring and dissembling forces of authority.

On-screen broadcasting interaction and sociability

So it seems that one of the key strategies of informalizing news is the choreographed 'banter' between co-presenters, and we now look at the importance of the news interview. As Heritage (1985) and Scannell (1996) have pointed out, the talk produced by all participants in news interviews is not just for each other, but also, and primarily, for the 'overhearing' audience. Even where there is a co-present (studio) audience there to observe, they may only participate under very close supervision (Higgins, 2008: 53). At their core, news interviews, whether they take place in a studio or are a vox pop in the street, are for the benefit of the absent audience rather than for the interviewer.

In normal conversation, certain rules are observed, such as the use of adjacency pairs whereby some utterances expect an appropriate response. Harvey Sacks puts it rather obliquely:

> By conditional relevance of one item on another we mean: given the first, the second is expectable; upon its occurrence, it can be seen to be a second item to the first; upon its non-occurrence, it can be seen to be officially absent – all this provided by the occurrence of the first item.
>
> (Sacks, 1992)

This can be illustrated by a relatively simple example, whereby a summons carries the adjacency pair of an answer:

A: Bert? [a summons item; obligates other to answer under penalty of being found absent, insane, insolent, condescending, etc.]

B: Yeah? [answers summons, thereby establishing availability to interact further. Ensures there will be further interaction by employing a question item, which demands further talk or activity by summoner.]

(Sacks, 1992)

There are a number of tasks being undertaken by this exchange. As we say above, the summoner wishes to verify the presence and availability of the interlocutor, but just as importantly the exchange also provides a means of opening the exchange that is to come. We can compare this with the forms of sociability we see on broadcast news. This is the manner in which presenter John Humphrys introduces the BBC Radio 4 morning news programme *Today*:

> JH: It's six o'clock on Friday the thirty first of August (.) good morning this
> is *Today* with Evan Davis and (.) John Humphrys

This is a greeting offered by Humphrys to the listening audience. It is implausible to suppose that Humphrys words would be able to elicit a response (a 'good morning' in return) that would confirm the attention and availability of the audience, like the summons to Bert highlighted by Schegloff. However, the greeting does provide an appropriately sociable manner of opening the series of addresses that are to come. Importantly, this presenter-to-audience relationship is only one of the axis along which broadcasting sociability operates. This is an exchange from the BBC Radio 4 evening news programme *PM*, where presenter Eddie Mair introduces an update on news from Cairo:

> EM: Our world affairs editor (.) John Simpson (.) is in Cairo (.) it's quite a
> day John
>
> JS: Eddie it's a remarkable day

Here, we see the presenter, Eddie Mair, shifting from addressing the overhearing audience with information on the whereabouts of the world affairs editor ('Our world affairs editor (.) John Simpson (.) is in Cairo') to opening an exchange with the journalist on location ('it's quite a day John'). The latter part of Mair's contribution is what Scannell (1991) describes as 'doubly-articulated'. It sets out the importance of an exchange between two on-air journalists, 'it's quite a day, John', in a manner that is designed to benefit an overhearing audience. Similarly, in the context of the programme, John Simpson's report is delivered to Mair, but with the purpose of giving a report to the listeners. There are therefore elements of the report that are explicitly sociable in the direction of the audience (greeting them to the programme, for example) and other elements where the audience are invited to behold the enactment of sociability between the on-air professionals.

Voices in news broadcasting

It seems, then, a significant factor in broadcasting news is the incorporation of voices, whether that be on the basis of expertise, first-hand experience, or ordinariness. In a moment, we will go on to look at another crucial item in the broadcast journalism toolbox: the news interview. First, however, Montgomery (2007: 144) provides useful categories for us to analyse the voices we hear on news reports. Aside from the main news presenter, there are four other categories we should think about:

- The experiential interview. Here, the interviewee can be an eye witness to an event, or as mentioned in the Introduction, the relative of soldier killed on active duty. We will see examples of such interviews in the report we will examine towards the end of the chapter.
- The expert interview. In such interviews, the interviewee is often presenting an expert opinion, such as a doctor who is being interviewed in association with a new health warning, or a university politics professor being interviewed about election results. Often too, such interviews are conducted with whatever professionals are involved with a news story, such as the policeman at the scene of the news story above.
- The affiliated interview. This interview is most often between the news presenter and a colleague who specializes in a certain area, such as health or business. We saw an introduction to such an interview in the exchange between Evan Davis and Adam Brimelow.
- The accountability interview. It is the accountability interview that we will turn to in a moment. Here, the interviewee is institutionally authoritative and can thus be held to account for the actions of a relevant body, such as a cabinet minister can be held accountable by the interviewer for government policy, or a company chief executive for a sharp decline in that company's profits.

These interviews do very different sorts of work in the news programme. Experiential interviews often provide emotional 'bystander' accounts. As Montgomery (2007: 178) says, 'in marked contrast to the accountable interviewee, [bystanders] are presented to the audience in a way that offers possible points of identification (or dis-identification), along the lines of – "yes; that is how I felt or how I might feel in their position", or even "that's not how I felt".'

Broadcast exchange rituals: arguments and sociability

We have said a great deal about the imperative towards sociability, and how this influences broadcast journalism. We will now look at the particular forms of sociability in the news interview. Turn-taking is a central element of spoken interaction. However, in multi-party conversation, there is the potential for chaos. Fortunately, as Deborah Cameron (2001: 91) describes, there are rules which exist to minimize this possibility in normal conversation. Such rules include:

> The current speaker selects the next speaker
> Or if this mechanism does not operate then …
> The next speaker self selects
> Or if this mechanism does not operate then …
> The current speaker may continue.

In media interviews, however, these rules of ordinary conversation do not apply. In such events, turn-taking is usually institutionally predetermined (Heritage and Greatbatch, 1991), where the interviewer has the pre-allocated role to ask questions while the interviewee is confined to offering direct responses. A further point is that the media news interviewer does not usually express his or her own perspective or personally react to statements made by the interviewee. In order to maintain impartiality, the interviewer usually does not express surprise or shock. However, as we will see later in the chapter, the interviewer may adopt an alternative, antagonistic view to provoke the interviewee's response.

Broadcast media talk also differs from ordinary conversation in the manner in which it is sequenced. Sequencing is the order in which speakers contribute and the roles they adopt, and in ordinary talk this is not usually predetermined. As Andrew Tolson (2006: 16) has observed, sequencing is particularly significant in media talk because it is so institutionally circumscribed. Roles are pre-allocated, such that someone will be the interviewer, the caller, the contestant, or the interviewee: roles which predetermine the contribution they are empowered to make.

Another of the characteristics of ordinary talk that distinguishes it from broadcasting is the long sequences of openings and closings. For example, in the case of a telephone call, the following would not be unusual (adapted from Hutchby 2006):

1. [telephone rings]
2. Nancy: Hello?
3. Hyla: Hi
4. Nancy: Hi
5. Hyla: How are you?
6. Nancy: Fine, how are you?
7. Hyla: Ok
8. Nancy: Good. What's doing?

In this prolonged opening sequence, the telephone's ring acts as the summons (lines 1–2). There is a process of identification and recognition (lines 2–4), including a greeting and acknowledgement (lines 2–4). This is extended in lines 5–8 until we reach the purpose of the call on line 8. As Hutchby (1996) points out, in most broadcast phone-ins involving members of the public, the first two moves in this sequence are unnecessary. In radio phone-ins in particular, the identity of the caller is announced by the host and the sequence is further curtailed by a much briefer exchange of greetings. The caller will then proceed to state an opinion without further prompting on the topic of the programme as the purpose of the call is clear from the context. A further characteristic of broadcast talk in this respect is the absence of a mutually negotiated closing sequence. The host has the institutional power to terminate the call – even cutting the caller off mid-sentence if it is thought appropriate.

In the case of most radio phone-ins that are predicated on confrontation (such as commonly found on 'shock jock' programmes and sometimes Radio 5 Live), Hutchby suggests the following four phases apply:

First phase: announcement and greetings.

Second phase: extended turn in which the caller states an opinion.

Third phase: host argues with that statement, followed by a relatively free exchange of speaking turns. Disputed points usually make 'good' tv or radio.

Fourth phase: the final turn, the host initiates the closing which may be as minimal as 'thank you'.

The host has the final say, giving them the most powerful position in the interaction. In the third phase, they may introduce the argument and, as Hutchby points out, the caller is invariably treated as 'arguable'. The sequential effect is of 'opposition-insistence' and talk is orientated towards this. The caller's 'first position' in the sequence is always vulnerable as it can be argued against by the host. The host is able to employ a formulaic strategy to display this power – 'You say X but what about Y?' While we can see, this is a form of exchange, callers are therefore forced onto a defensive footing. This applies as much to the radio phone-ins of Hutchby's data as to news interviews with those in institutional power (Montgomery's 'accountability' interviewee [2007]). As has been suggested elsewhere (Schiffrin, 1984), banter and light-weight teasing are elements which contribute to a sociability in argument. We find examples of this in many radio phone-ins.

Yet, in spite of these rigid structures of interaction and the arrangements of power, it remains that broadcast sociability is an important element of many radio and television journalistic programmes. As Scannell points out:

> The relationship between broadcasters, listeners and viewers is an unforced relationship because it is unforceable. Broadcasters must, before all else, always consider how they shall talk to people who have no particular reason, purpose or intention for tuning on the radio or television set.
>
> (1996: 23)

Even where it lapses into confrontation between interactants, broadcast journalism is obliged to be agreeable to the audience. As we saw above, the use of argument and confrontation can be a vital element in audience engagement. Yet, even when there is no direct audience link through phone-ins or live studio audiences, broadcast sociability can be maintained through subtle linguistic strategies such as the use of pronouns. This is illustrated in the following short extract taken from a BBC Radio 2 programme, *The Jeremy Vine Show*, which features a studio discussion between the presenter, Jeremy Vine (JV), and studio guests (TL and PL) (see Table 2.8).

Table 2.8

JV	Mr Leechy and his wife Paula are both with me in the studio	1
	now here on Radio 2 (.) as is their interpreter (.) Susan Booth	2
	(.) whose voice you will hear (.) Welcome to you both and	3
	thanks for coming in.	4
TL & PL	Hello	5
JV	Can you just tell us first of all (.) Paul (.) about your child and	6
	how you felt when you discovered she was deaf?	7

Awareness of the absent listening audience is shown initially in the contextualizing information the presenter gives (lines 1–2), to explain how there are three other people in the studio with him, but that the main voice we will hear is of their interpreter (the two main participants are both deaf). The studio is treated as a social space, where the guests are welcomed and thanked for 'coming in' (lines 3–4), helping to create a sense of ownership between broadcaster and listener. Vine shifts his use of the second person pronoun 'you' in line 3 from the inclusive direction towards the overhearing audience ('voice *you* will hear') to the exclusive salutation to his studio guests ('welcome to *you*'), although oddly he is also excluding the interpreter, Susan Booth, through his focus on Tim and Paula. Vine then aligns himself with the overhearing audience in line 6 when he asks the guests to 'tell *us*', and thus includes them in the discussion. The audience at home are thereby invited to listen-in on an exchange at which they are not present, but it is made clear that it is for *their* benefit that the interaction is produced.

News interviews

Interactivity in the form of interviews between journalists/news presenters and others is increasingly being seen as vital to news reporting. The monologic report we have analysed above from Kate Adie was determined by the limits of technology at least as much as by journalistic convention. However, in terms of where things are headed, Hutchby comments:

> Increasingly, the more interactive formats of broadcast news are coming to outweigh the monologic contributions of the standard newsreader [...] Key agenda-setting news broadcasts such as BBC radio's *Today* programme or BBC tv's *Newsnight* routinely consist of a series of interviews, each prefaced with little more than a brief contextualising statement by one of the [presenters].
>
> (2006: 121)

We have approached these developments through a focus on artful informality. Sometimes this is visible, such as the less formal clothing in-the-field reporters wear to make their reports on television news. Elsewhere can be seen in a marked decrease in deference, where the journalist assumes an adversarial approach to their questioning.

If we begin by looking at how 'ordinary' language uses questions, we will see how different journalistic interviewing styles can turn out to be. In ordinary conversation, we tend to ask questions in order to seek clarification or information. For example,

Chris: How's your foot?
Tony: Oh, it's healing beautifully
Chris: Good

As we can see, Chris's second turn acknowledges Tony's answer in a format we can describe as question-answer-acknowledgement. Slightly different to this is the use of language in the classroom where power relations are in operation:

Teacher: Can you tell me why you eat food?
Pupil: To keep you strong.
Teacher: To keep you strong. Yes. To keep you strong.

Here, the teacher's response to the pupil's answer forms an evaluation, and thus we have a format of question-answer-evaluation in operation. What we see in journalistic news interviews is somewhat different. For one thing, it is far less likely that the interviewer will use back channels such as 'Mmh' and

'Yes'. Also, the topic is defined by the news organization, not the journalist or the interviewee. Hutchby (2006: 126) suggests that the reason for this is twofold. Firstly, the primary recipient of the talk is the overhearing audience, not the interviewee and therefore less attention needs to be paid to such rules of politeness as allowing the interlocutor to stick to topics that will allow them to maintain 'face'. The interviewee is usually complicit in this orientation towards the overhearing audience, as they will rarely produce talk that is designed for the interviewer's hearing only. Secondly, it is not uncommon for news interviews to be edited for use in later bulletins where a 'clean' copy (i.e. one without the context-specific questions, interventions and responses of the interviewer) is necessary. What this amounts to, according to Hutchby, is that:

> The political interview is not only a mediated phenomenon in its own right –
> that is, a form of interaction that takes place in the public domain, mediated
> by radio, TV or newspapers. Sometimes, what happens is an interview
> becomes 'newsworthy' itself.
>
> (Hutchby 2006: 134)

The main sort of news interview we will be looking at is the accountability interview (Montgomery 2007: 146). Such interviews feature people who are public figures with some kind of responsible role in relation to a news event, and can therefore be held 'accountable' in some way. Montgomery has observed that 'accountability interviews develop out of a news item but also have the potential to feed into subsequent coverage – particularly by providing a topical resource in the form of quotation for a later news item' (2007: 153). He offers the interesting example of an interview former British Prime Minister Tony Blair gave to the Al Jazeera *Frost over the World* programme on 17 November 2007 (see Table 2.9).

Table 2.9

Blair	[The Iraqi people want] the same opportunities and the same rights	1
	that we enjoy in countries such as this.	2
Frost	But but so far it's been (1.5) you know (.) pretty much of /a disaster/	3
Blair	/it it it it /	4
	HAS but you see what I saw to people is (.) why it is difficult in Iraq	5
	[...]	6

The following day, the global media reported this interview in a way that implied Blair had used this interview to declare that the invasion had proved to be a disaster:

> Iraq is a 'disaster' admits Blair (*Daily Mail*, 18 November)
> Iraq invasion a disaster, Blair admits (*Daily Telegraph*, 18 November)
> Blair's 'Iraq disaster' interview provokes storm (CNN)
> Blair admits Iraq 'a disaster' (Al-Jazeera)
> Blair accepts 'disaster' in Iraq (BBC online)

However, if we look at the transcript of the actual interview, we can see Blair begins to talk before Frost has finished speaking (line 4), and it is the interviewer Frost's words that characterize the invasion as a disaster, even then hedging the description with 'pretty much of …'. What we should note, however, is that Blair does not use the word 'disaster' himself, but merely acknowledges that as an acceptable interpretation ('it HAS'). Thus, in holding interviewees to account, this is an interview style that allows a substantial degree of interpretative scope for the journalist:

> Not only may the interview be held to account within the interview for actions and words prior to it, but the interview may generate material that can be used subsequently for accountability purposes.
>
> (Montgomery 2007: 155)

'Neutralism' and challenging questions

The hazards that Montgomery alludes to may well be one of the reasons why so many politicians avoid accountability interviews, usually with the evasive turn of phrase that they are 'not available for comment'. Nevertheless, the currency of the accountability interview as a journalistic exercise remains high, and the position of high-performing interviewers as 'tribunes of the people' (Clayman, 2002) or 'public inquisitors' (Higgins, 2010) require that traditional norms of sound journalism are maintained. With this in mind, Clayman (1988) uses the term 'neutralism' to reflect the manner in which journalists' questions do not betoken a personal viewpoint but nevertheless challenge the interviewee.

Part of the way this is done is through the strategy of footing shift. This builds on work by Goffman (1981). As Hutchby shows, a speaker may adopt one of three footings:

Animator :   the producer of an utterance.

Author: the person whose words are actually being uttered (e.g. speech writer, a letter writer).

Principal: the person whose viewpoint, stance, beliefs, etc., the utterance expresses (e.g. a judge's words in a court judgement).

(adapted from Hutchby 2006: 127)

As Clayman (1992) argues, the use of footing shift enables the interviewer to fulfil two professional tasks simultaneously: to be adversarial, while remaining formally neutral. Yet, argues Clayman (1992), this neutrality is actually a position of truth-seeker on behalf of 'the people' over whom the power is being exercised. As both Clayman (2002) and Higgins (2010) note, this is a discursive position that warrants performances of aggression, acting on the public's behalf, that would be untenable in ordinary conversation.

We can see examples of these features in an interview by John Humphrys, the presenter of the BBC radio news programme *Today*. He is seen here (Table 2.10) interviewing the Defence Secretary Des Browne in light of a High Court ruling that appears to suggest British armed service personnel have inadequate equipment and that the government is legally accountable for this.

Table 2.10

JH	Let me ask you first why and presumably you do accept that the High	1
	Court ruled that soldiers were sent to war without the right equipment	2
	can sue the government using the Human Rights Act (.) you do accept	3
	that that was part of the ruling?	4

Here, Humphrys is seen to shift footing from being his own author in the first phrase on line 1 ('let me ask you first why') into the footing of an animator whose principle is actually that of his interviewee ('presumably you do accept …') before shifting again to the footing where the author is the high court judge's words ('soldiers were sent to war …'). This strategic play for neutrality allows the interviewer to switch between topics.

This interview also includes formulations by both participants. Formulations are inferentially elaborative probes which allow the interviewer to cast events in a way that may imply a different interpretation. In Table 2.11, we can see the presenter (JH) formulating events leading up to the interview in a way that makes the government appear to have acted in an unfavourable light, whilst the interviewee (DB) contests this formulation, wording the events in a more constructive manner:

Table 2.11

JH	You went to the court to stop the coroner of accusing the MOD of	1
	serious failures that is a fact	2
DB	No no no John I didn't try to /stop	3
JH	/ What did you do then?/	4
DB	the investigations/ will you please let	5
	me answer the question? I didn't try to stop these investigations I mean	6
	in fact I encourage these investigations and we support these	7
	investigations and I direct support for them from the heart of the MOD	8
	every single day (.) I raise the issue of cooperating with these	9
	investigations these inquests and we welcome these inquests (.) what we	10
	did in one of the seven points which were raised six of which were	11
	raised by em the the family in this particular case we on the advice of	12
	lawyers asked the court to give direction in relation to two words which	13
	were used by the coroner.	14

Humphrys's initial declarative statement is directed at Browne by means of the second person pronoun 'you', indicating it is Browne's own actions rather than his position of institutional accountability that are being challenged in this interview; a formulation that is repeated in Humphrys's next turn. Browne responds by attempting to reformulate this himself by using the collective first-person pronoun 'we' (line 10 onwards) to imply collective responsibility. This distancing from personal responsibility is taken further by the mention of the action being taken on legal advice (lines 12–13). Finally, Humphrys's unmitigated 'to stop' is downplayed by Browne into 'asked' (line 13), which implies a less high-handed approach to this matter. Thus, what analysis of the accountability interview enables us to do is to see how interaction in broadcast journalism is strategic in character, and dedicated towards presenting and contesting interpretations of the truth, while attending to such professional norms as neutrality.

Broadcast news: managing the extraordinary and the ordinary

The accountability interview is an extreme manifestation of an artful use of interaction that we find throughout broadcast journalism. We will now look at how interaction can pervade the management of an extended news report. What follows (Extract 1) is an extract from an evening news broadcast, reporting on the murder and assault of a British family in France in September 2012. The extract includes the headline sequence, followed by the opening words of one the main newscasters (see Table 2.12):

Table 2.12 ITV1, 7 September 2012, extract 1.

	[Headlines]	1
AS	The terrifying ordeal of two sisters (.) as their family is gunned	2
	down in France (..) one child sheltered on the floor of <u>this</u> car (.)	3
	the other slumped into the hands of a rescuer (..) but why were their	4
	parents and grandmother murdered?	5
		6
Translator	The role of an investigator is to find out what happened (..) but this	7
	is an act of <u>extreme</u> savagery	8
		9
Voice over	This is the ITV evening news (.) at six thirty (.) with Alastair	10
	Stewart and Mary Nightingale	11
		12
MN	The girls' father was <u>Iraqi</u> born his business involved satellites (.)	13
	whether that prompted a professional <u>hit</u> (.) or it was an <u>armed</u>	14
	<u>robbery</u> that went wrong (..) among the leads the French police are	15
	pursuing tonight	16
		17
	[...]	18
AS	Good evening she had seen her mother (.) father and grandmother	19
	shot <u>dead</u> in their car and her sister beaten within an <u>inch of her life</u>	20
	(..) yet (.) a four year old British girl had to wait another <u>eight</u>	21
	<u>hours</u> before police in <u>France</u> found her (..) she was hiding under	22
	the legs of her dead <u>mother</u> (..) after a <u>shooting</u> in the <u>French</u> Alps	23
	that has <u>baffled</u> the police	

It is apparent that elements of the structure of the story have things in common with the inverted pyramid model we see in newspapers. The headline performs many of the same functions as a conventional lead sentence, specifying what happened and where. The newest detail to emerge – the discovery of the youngest sister in the car, after the survival of her older sibling – offers the hook for the story. The headline centres on the traumatic experience of this victim, with the incident itself presented as a presupposition ('as their family is gunned down …'). A similar emphasis, referring the events through the senses of the victim, is then repeated in the opening segment of the main section (lines 19–20). The implication is that the audience will already know that the incident has occurred, and be in search of detail; provided here through an account from the (imagined) perspective of one of the victims.

Where this extract differs from print is in the capacity for performance: to distribute emphasis (marked by underlining) to place stress on the drama of the crime (professional hit, armed robbery, within an inch of her life, shooting), as well as emphasize severity (extreme savagery, dead) and familial relations (mother). It is therefore easy to see how a combination of the narrativization of the events – in particular, emphasizing the participants – and the careful use of emphasis allow us to gather a sense of the newsworthiness of the events. The colloquial nature of the language (e.g. 'gunned down' on line 2 and 'within an inch of her life' on line 20) used also creates a sense of intimacy and accessibility for the viewers. This is enhanced as the opening headlines are concluded with a response-demanding utterance ('but why were their parents and grandparents murdered?' line 5).

Just as the voice of the presenter, with all its stresses and subtleties, distinguishes broadcast journalism from older print forms, so the technology of broadcasting presents increasing scope to bring in a variety of participants, as this next extract (Table 2.13) begins to show:

The first of the outside voices we hear is an institutionally sanctioned one, when Mary Nightingale signals a temporary handover to European correspondent Emma Murphy. Murphy's voice appears over footage, and she anchors her position as part of the scene through the use of deictic pointers 'this road' and 'this cover'. Murphy then gives way to the professional voice of the policeman (captioned on screen and voiced through a translator), followed by two holidaymakers from the campsite at which the victims had stayed. This use of what Bonner (2003) has called 'ordinary people' to place the story in context continues in this following extract (Table 2.14):

Table 2.13 ITV1, 7 September 2012, extract 2.

MN	The family was from Surrey (.) Saad and Iqbal Al-Hilli who came	1
	to Britain from Iraq were on a caravanning holiday with their two	2
	<u>daughters</u> and Mrs Al-Hilli's <u>mother</u> (.) it ended with bullets to the	3
	head (.) not just to the <u>family</u> but also for a passing cyclist (..) our	4
	Europe correspondent (.) Emma Murphy (.) reports	5
		5
	They had driven up this road (.) a family enjoying a holiday (.) they	6
EM	were driven back down in <u>body</u> bags and <u>vans</u> (..) <u>four</u> lives	7
	snuffed out in an act described as gross savagery	8
		9
	What I can tell you at the moment is that three of the four people	10
Translator	killed were struck by shots to the head (…) we'll have to wait for	11
for police	the result of the autopsy from Grenoble (.) but <u>three</u> of the four	12
	were shot in the head (..) the role of an investigator is to discover	13
	what <u>happened</u> (.) but it is an act of <u>extreme</u> savagery	14
		15
	Beneath this cover at the far end of the path is Al-Hilli family	16
EM	BMW (..) Saad died in the driver seat (.) his wife Iqbal in the back	17
	(.) beside the grandmother (..) and on the ground just beyond (.) a	18
	French cyclist's life ended (.) possibly <u>shot</u> for what he saw (…)	19
	and amidst the scenery and the savagery (.) two little girls (..) an	20
	eight year old beaten so <u>badly</u> it was thought she was dead (.) and a	21
	four year old so <u>terrified</u> (.) that she cowered beneath her dead	22
	mother's legs so still that for <u>eight hours</u> no one knew she was	23
	there	24
		25
	The girl was discovered <u>completely</u> immobile (.) in effect <u>buried</u> in	26
Translator	the vehicle (.) behind the front passenger seats (.) under the legs of	27
for police	one of the dead women (.) under skirts and bags (.) completely	28
	invisible and not making a sound	29
		30
	The family have been staying at the Solitaire du Lac camp site (.)	31
EM	near Lake Annecy	32
		33
	Just normal people (.) normal children (.) and they were just	34
First camper	<u>playing</u> (.) the children	35
		36
	The people were on holiday (.) y'know (.) it's fun here (.) and	37
Second	somebody else (.) in the mountains (.) is crazy	38
camper		39

The dynamic between the place of the studio as the site of control and institutional sanction (see figure 2.1) and the various locations as sites of liveness and authenticity (see figure 2.2) is emphasized by the shifts in broadcast setting. There are a number of points regarding this use of non-professional or

Figure 2.1

Figure 2.2

specialist interviewees that are worth thinking about. The first is the quantity of such interviewees. Across the scene of the crime and the village in which the family live, five voices are introduced of which two, GA and JS, have particular knowledge of the family. Also, the sense of unscriptedness across these contributions is striking. Markers of hesitancy are prominent; and a number of the interviews are edited to include the interviewees expressing

Table 2.14 ITV1, 7 September 2012, extract 3.

JB	Neighbours were struggling to believe that a family from this small	1
	town in Surrey had been so ruthlessly executed during a summer	2
	holiday (..) this is stockbroker belt Surrey (.) quiet and affluent (.) it	3
	was here that Saad Al-Helli (.) his wife (.) and two daughters (.)	4
	called home (…) George Aicolina lives <u>two doors</u> away and chatted	5
	regularly with the family (.) who <u>originally</u> came from Iraq	6
		7
	I had a tremendous shock and I am in a way speechless (.) and	8
Neighbour,	emotionally shaken (.) ehm (.) because I have known him for a	9
George	period of time and I never thought (.) something of this kind would	10
Aicolina	happen to him and his family	11
		12
	Jack Saltman was looking after their property while they were	13
JB	away (.) he said Saad (.) who trained a satellite engineer (.) had	14
	confi<u>ded</u> in him about <u>problems</u> (.) but he <u>wouldn't</u> expand	15
		16
	Err (..) he said <u>one thing</u> that may or may not be of significance and	17
Friend, Jack	I <u>have</u> passed that onto the police so I couldn't say anything more	18
Saltman	than that	19
		20
	Saad Al-Hilli was fifty years old (.) although <u>originally</u> from Iraq	21
JB	he was a <u>British</u> citizen (..) he was a director of a company called	22
	<u>SHTECH</u> (.) that designed computer software (..) he was also	23
	associated with a Wiltshire based aerial photography company (.)	24
	eight year old Zeinab went to the local primary school (.) her little	25
	sister (.) Zeena (.) would have started there this term (..) parents	26
	were told of the tragedy	27
		28
	It just feels wretched (.) erm cause I've got a little girl here and a	29
Parent	little boy (.) and just to obviously hear the reports on the news on	30
	the radio that erm (.) what's (.) happened to the other little girl is	31
	just absolutely awful	32
		33

their inability to translate their feelings into words. The main concern of the other interviewees is the ordinariness of the family and, particularly on the part of the 'parent', a sense of empathy.

Importantly, through the correspondent Juliet Bremner, this ordinariness is explicitly bound up in location, 'this small town in Surrey […] this is stockbroker belt Surrey'. Related to this is the relationship between national identity and place that pervades the report. In keeping with the expectation that the place of a news story be made clear at the outset, the headline (table 2.13) places the scene in France. The opening contribution of the main report specifies the (as yet, unnamed in the broadcast) victims as British, before emphasizing that the police – during an implied criticism – are French and emphasizing again the foreign locale.

It is apparent that such news stories use language choice and strategies of emphasis to highlight the salient aspects of the story and to amplify its emotive qualities. We can also see that location and identity have a role in guiding and substantiating the emotionality of the story. What is also apparent is the extent to which these are a number of factors that contribute to an overall discourse of ordinariness that draws heavily upon unscripted and emotionally expressive contributions from non-institutionally sanctioned laypeople.

The multi-modality of broadcast news

As a communicative activity, it is crucial that we see journalism as 'multi-modal' (Kress and van Leeuwen, 2001). Brian Baresch, Shih-Hsien Hsu and Stephen Reese (2012: 644) state the challenge badly as one of sustaining an overarching interpretation on 'developing digital journalistic forms such as interactive graphics and other data visualisations'. As we note in our discussion of the BBC Sport online provision, the broadcast delivery of news therefore presents any viewer or listener with an expanding range of aural and visual stimuli, all incorporable to varying extents into the consumption experience. Added to this, as the technical affordances of news delivery platforms increase in sophistication, so it is that more modes of information can be contained in the product. As an illustrative example of the opportunities for analysis this multi-modality offers, this is an image of a news broadcast from international rolling news channel *Russia Today* (Figure 2.3):

There are a variety of communicative activities on screen here, all of which perform particular connotative duties and which combine to establish and maintain the institutional credibility that underpins each of the journalistic items delivered. The most obvious dynamic is that between the word and image, and here we see that the affordances of television and online platforms are deployed in the backscreen projection of images from the story read by the newsreader (A), on the successful landing of a stricken aeroplane. Second,

Figure 2.3 Russia Today, 18 August 2019.

as Cushion and Lewis (2010) point out, rolling news channels proceed on the basis of a rapid turnover of viewers switching in and out of the channel. The *Russia Today* broadcast makes it clear that viewers are watching the very latest news implicitly through the labelling of 'live' at the lower corner of the screen (B). This is common in news broadcasts, and helps to identify clearly and quickly that a broadcast is the latest, potentially breaking, news. Another feature that contributes to the comprehension of the viewer who has recently tuned in, and in order to enable a rapid appreciation of the item reported, is a headline for this main story 'Miracle Landing' which spans the bottom of the screen (C). Third, the claim of such rolling news to deliver material as it emerges is emphasized in brief news updates delivered along the bottom of the screen on the chyron, presented here as a news ticker (D). As is necessary in a constrained space, this text is written with the linguistic features normally found in a news headline, with the omission of function words. In this case, the news ticker text would formally be written as: 'Jeffrey Epstein's lawyers <u>are</u> to investigate <u>the</u> disgraced financier's death'. Fourthly, and just as importantly for the ambitions of the channel, the clock at the bottom left of the screen does not represent the time zone occupied by the viewer, but rather produces a rotating check on the times of major world cities, such as Berlin (pictured), London, Moscow and Tokyo (E). As well as anchoring whichever events may be unfolding in those places in their local context, this clock performs the far more important semiotic purpose of emphasizing, in this case, *Russia Today's* international reach and global pretentions.

There is a projection of breathless rapidity and timeliness that characterizes the representation of broadcast news, as the following screengrab from the Al Jazeera news channel shows (Figure 2.4):

Figure 2.4 Al Jazeera, 19 August 2019.

We will recognize many of the conventions identified in the image from *Russia Today*, including the story-related-backdrop. In the case of our Al Jazeera example, this is joined by the projected image of an expert interviewee engaging in a 'live two-way' discussion with the host in studio. In the Al Jazeera image, we see a further example of how what Natalie Fenton (2012) refers to as the combined demands of speed and increased capacity is embodied in the graphics. In particular, and evoking the *New York Times*-run zipper in Times Square, we see the news ticker scrolling the text along screen, recalling the traditions of 'breaking news' while accentuating the mood of breathless immediacy. One of the perils of this, however, is also revealed in this screengrab: only the text in the centre of the zipper is coherent, with the preceding and subsequent stories only appearing in incoherent extracts.

Conclusion

In this chapter, we have examined the particular forms of language that emerge in broadcast journalism. What characterizes broadcast journalism is the scope for embodied and/or expressive performance. Across both interviews and news broadcasts, we have seen how types of performance work to emphasize newsworthiness and engender emotional responses. The language of broadcast journalism is best understood in the fuller context of the broadcast setting: whether that is the performative conventionality of the studio, giving vivid expression of the scene of a newsworthy event, or empathizing amid the stricken and bereaved. Throughout, we have also been concerned how much broadcast news forms part of a drive in broadcast media towards 'sociability'. Within this context, we have also looked at the place of news values and impartiality, and at how these might attend to the need to engage the audience while participating in the professional activities of journalistic truth-telling. We have been concerned with the peculiar form of interactions of various forms of 'interview', looking, for example, at ways that journalists engage others in a potentially face-threatening manner, finding that the engagement with the audience is discharged by the journalists' speaking on the audience's behalf. Furthermore, we have looked at how a news report can incorporate this sense of interaction from within a studio setting, as well as drawing in outside journalists and other interactants, in a manner designed to emphasize news values and maximize emotional engagement. Finally, and importantly, we looked at how the multi-modality of the broadcast news production adds complexity and nuance to both the journalistic text itself and the possibilities of interpretation, in ways that we can see serve the priorities of the news organizations themselves. Later in this book, when we come to explore the linguistic features of Digital Journalism, we will see how the drive towards 'sociability' and immediacy is enhanced further.

3

Magazine journalism

Introduction

Magazines tend to be more specialized than we find in many other media platforms. Both the demographic qualities and the expected interests of magazine readers are thought through in detail and placed at the centre of how titles package and sell themselves. Because of these possibilities of specialization and the forms of reader appeal in which magazines engage, the normative conventions of journalistic practice that we see through other chapters apply less readily to magazines, including the expression of forms of affinity that would look out-of-place in other journalistic contexts. One of the strands that runs through journalism and that we will see amplified in magazines is the use and reproduction of a sense of community, whether that be driven by mutual interest, by shared beliefs or by a common national or regional identity. Indeed, as we proceed through this chapter, we come to understand a way of using language that extends beyond the maintenance of community and balances discourses of exclusion and inclusion: differentiating and setting apart their own communities of shared interest.

As befit the roots of the word itself as a 'storehouse', magazines are often characterized as department stores or repositories, filled with a diverse range of voices and discourses. If we are to extend this metaphor further, we could therefore claim that the cover of a magazine is its shop window. It has similarities with the front page of a newspaper, but as we will see in the next chapter, while newspapers produce the occasional iconic front page, their disposable and time-bound qualities demand a more immediate and transitory form of linguistic play than is required for the more leisurely reader of a magazine. Magazines also have a greater capacity to play with visual images, layout and graphology. The cover is a complex semiotic system that displays a variety of meanings through language, images, colours, fonts and placement. More than newspapers, the cover design of a magazine will distinguish one from another, which is particularly important when we consider the number of magazines that are available. A magazine is designed to stand out from the crowded shelves, and the magazine name is clearly visible in order to distinguish it from others at a glance.

As McCracken (1992: 15) notes in her classic textbook, the cover is regarded the most important page in a magazine from both an editorial and design perspective. As Johnson and Prijatel (1999: 240) argue, the cover is a magazine's face and 'it creates that all-important first impression. It also provides both continuity through format recognition and change through intriguing cover lines from issue to issue.' McCracken (1992: 19) has observed that 'the cover serves to label not only the magazine but the consumer who possesses it'. In this way, lifestyle magazines will commonly feature a bold image of a model or celebrity who the reader can aspire to be like, or to otherwise want to be associated with, along with bold claims that align with the consumer's own aspirations. There is some overlap across the news values we described in Chapter 1 and the qualities that are favoured in magazines. However, there are several differences and Johnson and Prijatel (1999: 240) offer the following as guidance:

- Photos sell better than artwork.
- Sex sells better than politics.
- Timeliness is a critical sales factor.
- Solutions sell better than problems.
- Subtlety and irony don't sell.
- Bylines don't sell.
- Puns don't work well in sell lines.

In this way, we can see that the cover of a magazine offers something different to a newspaper: the stress on content and its relevance may be more straightforward, and negativity plays a less prominent part. We will start by looking at how this shop window of a magazine, its cover, is put together before we move on to explore the content in more detail. This will involve looking in some detail at five different magazine covers (*Cosmopolitan, Men's Health, National Enquirer, Olive* and *Women's Health*). Out of necessity, these are reproduced here in black and white, but where appropriate, we will also make note of the use of colour.

Magazine titles and slogans

There is a pattern in the ways in which a magazine's title is located on the cover. As with all alphabetical texts, we will tend to read from top left to bottom right. This means that the reader is inclined to look to the top left of the page for the publication title. Because of the way in which magazines are usually displayed in shops, on racks that fan out from the left to the right to allow the consumer to pick up the publication by its spine, the importance of the left side of the cover is paramount. This is true of magazines as well as newspapers. However, there is a second similarity and that relates to colour and font. As we will explore in the next chapter, tabloids have a subcategory known as 'red tops', which relates to the red and white masthead used by newspapers such as *The Sun, The Mirror* and *The Star* in the UK. These lower-priced, celebrity-focused newspapers have equivalents in the magazine genre, where the same red-top (or deep pink and white) style is used in similarly orientated magazines such as *Take a Break* and *Best* in the United Kingdom, and *National Enquirer* in the United States. This style makes it easier for the purchaser to identify the sort of magazine they want to purchase by the style of masthead. As with the 'red tops', the semantic qualities of the publication can indicate its quality in other ways. In newspapers, as we shall see in the next chapter, the size of the paper is generally regarded as being an indication of its quality, with the smaller tabloid format being typical of the redtops, and the larger broadsheet size being used for the more 'serious' newspapers. In magazines, this distinction lies not in the size of the magazine (most of them are a standard size that has been the case for decades), but it is the quality of the paper itself. In this way, the more expensive magazines are colloquially known as 'glossies'. These often contain more pages than the redtops, and as such are typically bound with glue rather than staples, a quality that allows for the extra cover space in the form of the text space on the spine. This space conventionally carries the title and issue of the magazines, but also the space for the slogan or for more details of the magazine's content. For example, the August 2019 edition of *Cosmopolitan* (Figure 3.1) carries the usual slogan 'I am Cosmopolitan' (a slogan that plays on the magazine's name also being an aspirational adjective), and then the tag line that acknowledges the market position of the magazine: 'The No.1 Women's Glossy Magazine'. In the same month's *Men's Health* (Figure 3.2), the spine features the title of this edition's special issue 'The body issue' before the subheading 'Men built to perform, not to bedazzle'.

Figure 3.1 *Cosmopolitan.*

Figure 3.2 *Men's Health.*

To return to McCracken's point about the consumer of the magazine aligning themselves with the culture a lifestyle magazine embodies through association with an aspirational cover image, this is most frequently in the form of a celebrity. The cover of the issue of *Men's Health* shown here is focusing on male fitness, and the image is not a celebrity as such, but 'Triple Crossfit Games Champion' who is explicitly identified as 'Mat Fraser'. Elsewhere on the cover, at the top of the page, we find a list of sportsmen – Mark Cavendish, Mo Farah,

Nile Wilson and Wilfried Zaha – with Mat Fraser's name included in that list. In this way, the less familiar Fraser is being aligned with the more recognizable names of the internationally well-known sportsmen. This is a process known as **semantic engineering**, where the semantic properties of one set of signifiers (here, famous male athletes) are aligned with those of another to infer a shared meaning. The celebrity names act as a selling point for the magazine, and are the only names on the covers. This follows Johnson and Prijatel's point about 'bylines don't sell' (1999: 240), as it is not the journalist or columnist whose name appears on the cover, as is commonly found on newspapers.

Layout and graphology

To return briefly the text on the spines of *Cosmopolitan* and *Men's Health*, it is clear that both of these are taking advantage of the possibilities of colour printing. The slogan on *Cosmopolitan* is in bright pink, contrasting with the rest of the spine's text which is in black but matching the colour scheme of this particular edition's front cover. In the text on *Men's Health's* spine, the black text contrasts with a dark green print for the content slogan, which follows the muted shades of the front cover. From this, we can see that colour is used strategically to highlight aspects of the magazine but also to follow certain generic and gendered stereotypes.

Font sizes are also used strategically. As the 'shop window' to the content of the magazine, they are summarizing at a glance what is inside. In the issue of *Men's Health* we are looking at here, this content is summarized under four aspirational adjectives: Lean, Hard, Toned and Fast. Each of these is written in large bold, sans serif font. Each is subtitled with a more expansive two-line summary in smaller font but block capitals. This is in contrast with the cover of *Cosmopolitan*, where there are six different subheadings, all in block capitals and variously in black of white sans serif font against the rose pink background. The top-left and bottom-right subheadings mirror each other in having explanatory text in block capitals, whilst the other four text boxes all have lower case subtitles after initial capitals. These strategies allow for a more 'readable' cover, in that there is variation in size and font, but nevertheless a pattern to the structure of the page that avoids it looking untidy by obscuring the body of the central image.

As a redtop magazine, *National Enquirer*'s (Figure 3.3) cover is more like a traditional three-column newspaper with the right side of the page devoted to two separate stories, whilst the main images are a montage of famous faces that takes up the left and central parts of the page. The text is similar to that we see on *Men's Health*, in that the main subheadings are in lower case, whilst the

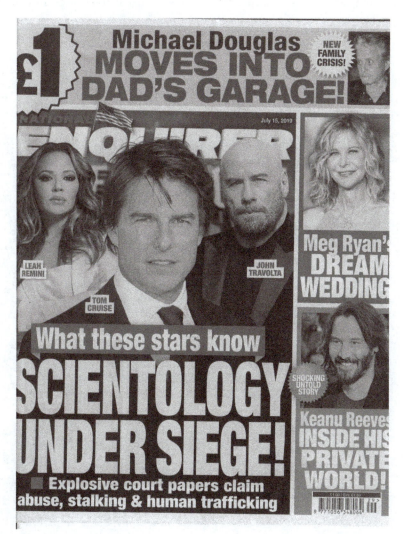

Figure 3.3 *National Enquirer.*

subtitles are in block capitals. There is a much wider use of colour in *National Enquirer*, which is typical of the bright and cheerful ethos of the redtops.

It is also the case that the fonts used can represent handwriting, as we can see on *Olive* (Figure 3.4) and *Women's Health* (Figure 3.5) covers. This adds variety to the cover design, helping to add an air of spontaneity and dynamism. In the case of *Women's Health*, the slogan across the bottom of the page – 'Your Best Summer Ever!' – looks like hand-painted text you might find on a beach hut, which is semantically aligned with the British notion of summer holidays. In the case of the text of *Olive*'s cover, this is restricted to the main

Figure 3.4 *Olive.*

Figure 3.5 *Women's Health.*

subheading – 'COLD DAYS, HOT FOOD' – which mirrors the sort of writing found on trendy restaurant menus. That both of these handwriting font pieces of text contain colour other than the black or white that is common on covers is another feature that aligns them with the overall cover design, as in both cases they feature the colour chosen for that edition's masthead.

The fact that the covers of magazines are designed to attract attention quickly means that there is a strong use of visual image, and where text does appear, it is in a font large enough to be read comfortably from a distance. This means the space devoted to such text is limiting its content, and so there are various linguistic strategies that have to be used to ensure that the message about the content is succinct but clear. This is what we shall now turn to.

Sentence types – main/minor

The magazine cover needs to cram a lot of information into a relatively small space, using font sizes that are sufficiently large to be read from a distance. Nouns can be extensively premodified, which is a feature of print language rather than spoken language. It serves to summarize a complex concept, and also help build the reader's anticipation of what is coming next.

Toxic stag parties – and the women paid to run them (*Cosmopolitan*, Figure 3.1).

Here, there is no finite verb. 'Paid' is a verb, but this is non-finite in this context because it not clear when the action is to take place (i.e. 'were paid' or 'are paid' or 'will be' all give three different tenses that are equally possible).

The best new gadgets for sculpting rock-hard abs (*Men's Health*, Figure 3.2).

Here again, there is no finite verb, and there is no subject to carry this out. The subject is generally the noun, noun phrase or pronoun that occurs before the verb. As readers, we need to actively read meaning into this minor sentence by inserting a pronoun and verb thus: '**These are** the best new gadgets for sculpting rock-hard abs.' In other words, we are actively engaging with interpreting the text.

Sometimes the modification comes after the head noun, such as in a post-modifying prepositional phrase. For example, the glossy food magazine *Olive*'s 'Chefs to watch this year' (Figure 3.4) comprises the head noun 'chefs' with the prepositional phrase that is modifying this to give the relevant information.

There is extensive use of elision and ellipsis, frequently omitted determiner. Adjectives are often used in place of determiners. For example, on the cover of *Olive*, addressing a reading position where the relevance of food is secure, there is a proliferation of elliptical phrases such as:

Cold days, hot food
Healthy comfort food that tastes great

Here, the main heading comprises the juxtaposition of cold/hot, in so doing setting up a problem and then offering the solution. The solution is expanded in the subheading with the head word *food* pre-modified with 'healthy comfort'. In both cases, these are minor sentences, heavily weighted in a recognizable lexicon of food, well-being and quality.

Minor sentences often lack a finite verb, but are complete in their intention. Finite verbs carry tense, such as present or past, which gives a clear idea of where something has been completed or when it took place. Because grammatical tense also is related to a subject, this verb can tell us whether an action refers to singular or plural participants.

Sentence functions – declaratives/imperatives/interrogatives, exclamatives

Imperatives appear to lack an explicit subject, but conventionally we understand them to implicitly include the interpreter as the subject. This lack of a specific subject gives a sense of timelessness to the text.

Exclamation marks are punctuation features that are routinely found on magazine front covers. They can be used to convey emotion, give a sense of immediacy and heighten a sense of involvement or inclusiveness for readers. If we think of these in terms of magazine news values, they generally add positivity to the magazine, usually containing a sentiment that is a solution to a perceived problem. For example, '2016's top trends revealed!' (*Olive*, Figure 3.4) implies the magazine is offering readers inside information on previously unknown developments in culinary excellence.

There is a tendency for the use of exclamation marks to be used with less frequency depending not on the linguistic content but on the market for the magazine. For example, if we look at the US-based celebrity gossip magazine, *National Enquirer* for July 2019, the cover features four stories, each of which carries an exclamation mark:

1. Michael Douglas moves into dad's garage!
2. Meg Ryan's dream wedding!
3. Keanu Reeves: inside his private world!
4. What these stars know: Scientology under siege!

In example 1, the exclamation is used to give a heightened sense of surprise: a famous film star is apparently reduced to living in a garage. This juxtaposition of celebrity and mundanity is the underlying surprise that the exclamation point is highlighting. The other examples are less remarkable in their content, with the exclamation mark being used instead to give a sense of immediacy, particularly in the case of example 4, where the Church of Scientology is frequently in the news for its practices, but here the exclamation point is indicating new information. Thus we can see that there is still an attention to positivity and excitement (examples 2 and 3 above), but there is also an additional excitement generated by scandal (examples 1 and 4). Gossip and scandal are more common tropes found in lower-priced magazines, irrespective of subject (news, lifestyle, hobbies, etc.).

In conventional spoken language, we use imperatives sparingly, but in print media, particularly in this case on magazine covers but also integral to advertising language, there is no problem with the absence of softeners such as 'please'. Delin (2000) points out that advertising language rarely uses 'please', and this is a feature of media language that is found on the front cover of magazines. The absence of this softening device acts to make us feel part of a community where the text producers have our best interests at heart and are enthusiastic in relaying this. It is to the creation of this sense of shared community that we will now turn as we look in more detail at the strategies magazines use inside their covers to create a sense of common understanding.

Magazines and synthetic personalization

In looking at how magazines use language to foster community, belonging and shared interest in readers, we will be drawing again on Norman Fairclough's concept of **synthetic personalization**, but focusing in this case on how the notion can be applied to written texts. Synthetic personalization is a way of describing how media text producers can employ linguistic strategies to encourage their audience to think of themselves as being addressed individually, while at the same time drawing them into a community of interest. As Talbot (2010: 151) explains, synthetic personalization has three facets: the establishment of commonality, the impression of two-way interaction and the use of informal language as a positive politeness strategy. The commercial underpinnings of this strategy are clear from its roots in the advertising language of the twentieth century, as well as its continuing pertinence to advertisers seeking to refine their forms of address (Vesanen, 2007). In fact, magazine language has many similarities with that found in advertising, drawing as it does on strategies of synthetic personalization. As Ellen McCracken has pointed out:

> The special-interest magazines often encourage their readers to think of themselves as members of a distinct group linked to certain modes of consumption [...] Because of their commercial goals, the special-interest publications address readers with messages of pseudo-individualised consumption linked to the ideological roles expected of members of such groups.
>
> (McCracken, 1992: 257)

Given the supposed differences in gendered consumption practices as well as discursive communities, we will be looking at how magazines aimed at women differ from those with a primarily male audience. To begin with, though, we will start by looking at certain linguistic features that are common in most magazines.

Common-sense assumptions

So what is the relationship between language and the construction of a community of readers? In his discussion of 'anti-languages', Michael Halliday (1975) shows how shared and exclusive vocabularies can separate and maintain a coherent social group: the construction of alternative vocabularies, shared used of metaphors. As Fairclough (1989) has observed, what are presented as 'common sense' interpretative schematics are required to make the fullest sense of many media texts. In other words, what do the participants in an exchange feel entitled to presume about each other's linguistic competence? In magazines, this can relate to the language used, such as abbreviations and elliptical references to the names of context-specific celebrities. Also playing a role are such conventional news values as recency and eliteness, as the magazines work to fashion their sense of community by referring to stories in previous issues, or by naming celebrities assumed are of specific interest to their readers (such as soap opera actors in many women's magazines and Premiership football players in magazines aimed at men). In this way, readers are drawn into a kind of complicity with the text. As Talbot (1995) observes, they are invited to silently acknowledge 'Oh yes – I remember hearing about that!', or call or reflect fondly on similarly expressed stories from past issues.

Another factor for us to consider is the multiple range of types of authorship we happen upon while leafing through magazines. As Talbot has pointed out:

> Magazines are not homogenous, and they never have been. Diversity is the key characteristic. They draw on a wide range of genres and discourses, addressing their readers in many different voices […] There is a consistent core of discourses and genres throughout magazines, which set up for readers consistent constellations of subject positions.
>
> (Talbot, 2010: 143–4)

While this is true to some extent of newspapers as well, these authors include not just the voices of journalists, but those of readers (through the letters' page and perhaps personal columns), interviewees, advertisers and special correspondents (such as problem page counsellors, health advisory writers and other experts), as well as an encouragement of distinctive and quirky writing styles in more general feature articles. Sometimes, there can be clashes in the assumed needs of the readers, such as advertising for 'anti-ageing' products running alongside articles about 'growing old gracefully', or features highlighting environmental concerns a few pages from a section of pieces on the glory of foreign travel. This runs deep in women's magazines in particular, as Schneider and Davis (2010) have explored in relation to diet and food in *Australian Women's Weekly*.

Many of these divergent voices and styles are determined by the particular genre into which the item falls. The following lists (Table 3.1) name some of the genres and discourse styles that routinely appear in lifestyle magazines for both men and women:

Table 3.1 Genres and discourse styles that routinely appear in lifestyle magazines for both men and women.

Genres	Editorial
	Letters page
	Instructional feature
	Advisory feature
	Fiction
	'True' stories
	Reviews
	Horoscopes
	Personal columns
	Advertisements
Discourses	Journalism
	Economics
	Family
	Fashion
	Science
	Feminism
	Sport
	Environmentalism
	Medicine and health
	Consumerism

The distribution and emphasis of these genres and discourses will depend on the magazine's editorial policy and the perceived audience. For example, women's magazines are routinely composed and edited with the assumption that readers will be interested in relationships and so will devote space to horoscopes and personal columns which combine the discourses of family, health and the empowering drive of feminism. Men's magazines, on the other hand, are more likely to call upon discourses of health and science using the discourse of the advisory feature. Also, it would be rare for a magazine directed at men to include horoscopes dedicated to offering advice on the personal life of the reader. In ways that we will explore in more detail shortly, this can be linked to a series of suppositions about gendered stereotypes.

Such underlying assumptions about differences between men and women can also underpin the more explicit common-sense assumptions found in magazines. There has been a lot of research into women's magazines (such as McCracken, 1992, and Talbot, 2010), supplemented by a growing body of work into men's magazines, with a particular focus on the development in the UK of mainstream magazines for younger men in the 1990s (such as Jackson, Stephenson and Brookes, 2001, and Benwell, 2003).

Long-standing gender stereotypes inform the content of such magazines in a largely unchallenged way. This involves a polarity of features which appear to produce '**two cultures**' view of male and female attributes (see Cameron, 2006). Clumsy as the oppositions may appear, these can be tabulated (see Table 3.2), drawing on the work of Jennifer Coates (1995, 1996) and Deborah Tannen (1991, 1995).

Table 3.2 Stereotyped male and female attributes.

Female	Male
Sympathy	Problem-solving
Listening	Lecturing
Rapport	Report
Connection	Status
Supportive	Oppositional
Intimacy	Independence
Cooperation	Competition
Submissive	Powerful

The topics that emerge from the application of these stereotypes to women cluster around a supposed interest in relationships and family, in sharing problems (intimate issues such as health and clothing) and issues such as domestic economy and management. For men, on the other hand, topics that prevail include competitive sport, muscle-building and toning, and individualizing technological gadgetry; all underpinned by a knowing humour that removes them from the realm of intimacy and into a more publicly generous performance of easy-going camaraderie. Whilst there had been a long tradition of magazines for men that covered specific topics or hobbies, there were very few successful general interest magazines in the same way as we find for women. This changed in the mid-1990s with the arrival of the so-called 'new lad', and highly successful introduction of magazines such as *FHM* ('For Him Monthly'), *Loaded* and *Maxim*. These were followed by weekly publications for an even more youthful demography: *Nuts* and *Zoo*, introduced in 2004, targeted young teens. However, changes in magazine consumption, with the arrival of free online content, from 2010 onwards led to declining print magazine purchasing across the spectrum. Whilst it seems women's magazines have retained their loyal readership, albeit with decreased circulation, the readership of 'lad's mags' virtually vanished, with the iconic *FHM* being the last to retreat to exclusively online content in 2016. We are left with a range of special-interest magazines, some of which are specifically aimed at men, such as *Men's Health*, but the differences in linguistic strategies between men's and women's magazines have now diminished considerably as the laddishness of the general-interest magazines such as *Loaded* and *FHM* retreated from print to online. For the purpose of this chapter, we will therefore explore just the general-interest magazines for women or for more general readers, as the linguistic features therein can also be extrapolated to the markers of solidarity that emphasize the **discursive community** of such magazine and the consumers who read and enjoy it.

Positioning the reader 1: the woke woman

To help us understand magazine journalism, we will begin by looking at the editor's letter from *Cosmopolitan* magazine to investigate how their communities of readers are created. As Brown and Gilman (1960) argue, the solidarity of much of the expression of community rests on the strategic use of such pronouns as 'you' and especially 'we'. In keeping with Fairclough's (2001: 52) theory of synthetic personalization – that is, a drive to address unseen mass audiences in the sympathetic tones of individual conversation – we will look at how pronouns are employed to include the reader, as well as at the role of presupposition and humour.

The first piece we will look at is the editor's address to the readers from the monthly woman's magazine, *Cosmopolitan,* a publication with a demographic target audience of women aged between 30 and 45 (Gauntlett, 2002). As we would find in most magazines, the editor's letter appears near the front of each issue. It performs the instrumental function of setting out the contents of that issue (in case a potential customer looks only at this page before making a purchasing decision), as well as serving as a greeting. It therefore provides a

FROM THE EDITOR

1. When I was 21 I left university with a shiny new degree, an encyclopaedic knowledge of mid-century French literature and … no job, no money and nowhere to live.

2. Still, I was lucky. My sister had a flat with an empty box room, so I hunkered down there for a while. I took a part-time job as a door girl at a London club in between work-experience shifts at magazines. Most nights I worked until five in the morning, peeling obliterated men and women from broken chairs, sticky floors and the arms (and loins) of unsuitables.

3. It was probably the poorest time of my lift. I had big student debts to pay off, a graduate loan and a maxed-out credit card. (No, hang on, make that two maxed-out credit cards.) Cash machines didn't appear to want to give me money. Neither did my bank manager.

4. Why am I telling you this? After all, this is some people's lives all of the time. I'm telling you to demonstrate what a very brief stint of poverty did to me. It made me do risky things.

5. I couldn't afford a cab home from work every night, so I took a lift with a man called Fred. I didn't know a thing about him. Not his surname, nor where he lived, nothing. He said he was a taxi driver and, rather more crucially, that he would drive me home across London every night for the price of a Big Mac and, frankly, that was good enough for me.

6. I couldn't afford a holiday either (I know, I know, first-world problems) so I accepted an all-expenses-paid trip to Hungary, offered by a tenuous acquaintance who had a friend of a friend of a friend who needed someone to do some 'copywriting' in Budapest over a weekend. So I flew out, found myself in a tower block with a man who looked like Meat Loaf, did the 'copywriting' (OK, it wasn't copywriting exactly but it was legal and it wasn't porn, so please don't worry), then came back to tell the tale to my horrified parents.

7. There are countless other misadventures I embarked on between the ages of 21 and 23. And yes, I do look back now and realise I was lucky, because the point where youth meets poverty is an opportunists' playground, filled with those who feed on the vulnerability and optimism of youth. Nowhere is this more acutely felt than in the UK's major cities, where the current rental crisis has given oxygen to a whole new breed of parasitic landlords. You can read Jennifer Savin's investigation of the young women sleeping with these men simply to secure a roof over their heads on page 98. It is frightening, it is unacceptable, and it needs to change.

Farrah x

FARRAH STORR

Editor

Cosmopolitan, March 2017

Figure 3.6 *Editor's letter from* Cosmopolitan, *March 2017.*

speech of welcome that helps to create a sense of community and engagement by highlighting topics that are presumed to be of shared interest. The issue we are looking at is for March 2017, and as such is a 'general' theme that does not tie into a seasonal issue, nevertheless it is calling upon the shared memory of the magazine and its readers. This is a shared memory that will include the assumption of a political engagement with issues of gender equality and 'shouting out' sexism, colloquially referred to as 'woke'.

Looking first at the layout of the page, it features a photograph of the editor, Farah Storr, whose name appears at the foot of the page in a position similar to that of a conventional letter. The photo shows the picture of a smiling woman, who appears to be enjoying the company of the reader with her relaxed, welcoming direct stare to camera. The setting suggests the outdoor seating area of a coffee shop, making this a sociable space. In this way, a sense of friendliness and sincerity is instantly created, factors which contribute strongly to what Brown and Levinson (1987) would describe as positive politeness.

An important component of the letter is how pronouns are used. If we take the first person pronoun, 'I', which appears in the first sentence and throughout this letter, we can see how this sincerity is built up in the text. Storr starts with an apparently random biography, detailing her early career after graduation as she worked in a series of low-paid jobs. This helps to connect her to readers who are likely to have had a similar experience of taking time to develop a career after university. Storr emphasizes her perilous financial state through an aside that appears in parenthesis. Such a strategy is a feature of conversational discourse, with the parenthesis acting as a confessional aside. Here, it replicates informal speech through the simulation of a self-correction: 'no, hang on'. In the context of print, this is strategic as the editing process allows for seamless correction, but in this case, it retains the spontaneous connotations of spoken language, and therefore appears more sincere. The use of parenthesis continues throughout this article, as it develops into a confessional story that links what appears to be a common experience of low-paid graduate employment into modern sexual exploitation as investigated in a feature that appears in this edition.

In the use of the second person pronoun, 'you', which appears in the fourth paragraph, we can see how this is directed at the readers of *Cosmopolitan*. This renders the readership more explicitly visible when it comes to be used as an **anaphoric referent** for 'some people' in the following sentence. The use of the question format for this first sentence in paragraph four appears to be in response to the unspoken question of the reader: 'Why is this relevant?' The letter continues with the unspoken questions of the reader being answered at various points, such as in paragraph six:

I couldn't afford a holiday either (I know, I know, first world problems) …

This is Storr's acknowledgement of a perhaps incredulous reader who is raising an objection to a self-pitying narrative of a younger Storr who is in employment and has safe accommodation (albeit not in the more affluent context of most readers of *Cosmo*). Her response is light-hearted, with the repetition of 'I know' to replicate spoken language, and then the acknowledgement that this lack of a holiday is a 'problem' only to those who are affluent.

She further adds to a sense of the knowing reader through her use of scare quotes. These is a print device that is used, according to Gaye Tuchman (1972: 135), as 'a signalling device'. Here, Storr uses them to provide a euphemism for potential sexual exploitation, which is legitimized linguistically as 'copywriting' but highlighted as being something other than this secretarial role through the use of the scare quotes. This is later expanded through an aside in parenthesis '(OK, it wasn't copywriting exactly but it was legal and it wasn't porn, so please don't worry)', to reduce the potential horror of such activities for vulnerable young women. To acknowledge the community of caring readers, Storr reassures her readers through the evocation 'don't worry'.

We will now continue to look in more detail at how these pronouns are used in relation to the discourses. If we begin by looking at the general 'female' community this magazine aims to construct, as implied by its title, then we can see that the editor's letter achieves this in a way that ties it in with the more specific 'moral' discourse explicitly advocated. The moral concerns that are central to this letter are validated in the fourth paragraph which contains the presupposition that this is common sense (triggered by the **idiom** 'After all, this is some people's lives all of the time'), and setting up the readers as part of a community of conscientious citizens. In terms of **news values**, this is validated through recency by the emphasis on this being a concern of 'the current rental crisis'. The wider community of women within which the magazine readership is implicitly situated is associated with theme of morality, particularly for young women, and the piece finishes with the tricolon that repeats the grammatical structure: 'It is frightening, it is unacceptable, and it needs to change'. This ties those concerns of the domestic and personal realm with matters of global import, themes that the magazine continues to build on.

This all adds up to a community that is closely aligned with wider national and global communities. The reader is assumed to be an active campaigner in line with the magazine's own editorial agenda. Here, the editor's letter is linking the 'housing crisis' of many UK cities (primarily those in the south of England, which is where most of the magazines have their main editorial offices), where low-paid female workers are highlighted as being particularly at risk of 'parasitic landlords'. Storr's own autobiographical narrative is presented as being 'lucky' to have escaped serious harm, but is linked to the experiences of young women who are not able to pay their rent, as found in a feature on page 98 of this magazine's edition. We can see here that despite the underlying negativity of the topic of sexual exploitation, there is an optimistic tone that links to a crusade on the part of the magazine to change things for better. In this way, the magazine editor's letter is following the general positivity that characterizes lifestyle magazines.

Magazine features

Most magazines have their most explicit journalistic content in the form of feature writing. There are many different varieties of such features, some of which are listed below:

- Service pieces, for example 'How to …'
- Inspirational, for example 'real life' stories of triumph over adversity
- Personal services, for example, make-overs
- Relationships
- 'Think' pieces, for example, documentary news reports
- Travel
- Reviews of books, music, film, etc.

- Interviews, often with celebrities
- Humorous items, particularly 'real life'
- Hobbies and sports, emphasizing the shared community of readers
- Nostalgia, for example, historical articles and biographies

(adapted from Hennessy, 1989: 61)

The type of feature included in a specific magazine will very much depend on the editorial stance of the publication and how it relates to the intended audience. For example, as mentioned above, magazines aimed at female readers, such as *Cosmopolitan, Marie Claire* and *Elle*, are likely to include features on relationships, lifestyle and inspirational personal experience, with celebrity interviews that will draw upon these themes. Magazines aimed primarily at male readers, such as *Men's Health* and *GQ*, will have features that place a greater emphasis on reviews, service pieces and interviews with celebrities from the field of sport or film.

In other chapters, we have noted how news stories have characteristic structures. Features are generally written to follow a structure of their own, as follows:

- Introduction
- Premise or point-of-view
- Thesis or frame
- Body (the core of points/arguments/explanations)
- Supporting material (anecdotes, quotations, etc.)
- Conclusion

(adapted from Hennessey, 1989: 36)

Added to this, the display on the page will differ from that of a newspaper in that it includes a title rather than a conventional headline, which is then followed by the standfirst (the sub-heading summarizing the article), followed in turn by the introductory paragraph. This is often accompanied by a large picture which frequently takes up most of the first page of a larger feature. Subject to the publication's house style, there is also routinely a creative use of font and colour to draw attention to the feature.

In addition to news values, there are other elements which contribute to the composition of a feature piece, as explained by Hennessey (1989), Davis (1995) and Delin (2000). These are evidentiality, coherence and point-of-view. We will look at these in more detail.

Evidentiality

Feature writing deals with colour or in-depth pieces in a more determinedly subjective manner (Evans, 1972; Higgins, 2006) and the evidentiality often depends more explicitly upon the credibility of the writer and other voices in the piece. Renowned or celebrity journalists or columnists give authority to a feature article, allied with the use of recognized sources. In large part, evidentiality is therefore established through these sources, and the greater the diversity of the sources, the stronger the argument. Such sources can include the testimonials of relevant participants or institutional expertise, as we saw with the experiential and expert interviews in news journalism. Sometimes, the authoritative source may be the acknowledged expertise of the writer. For example, a motoring correspondent or arts journalists would have a particular level of entitlement to write in their own voice. However, more routinely, features are based on independent research such as interviews, news cuttings, books and online resources.

Also, the diversity of sources which add weight to the authority of a magazine feature's evidentiality needs to be managed in such a way that their derivation remains clear to the reader. The more reputable or impressive a source is, the more beneficial it will be. So it is usually the case that lengthy noun phrases are used to introduce sources, pre-modifying a person's name with details of their authority, such as 'creative director of Chanel Cosmetics, Peter Phillips, tells me ...' (*Grazia*, 24 May 2010).

The words spoken or written by a source can be quoted in several different ways. A **direct quotation** in the form of direct speech can be managed within the feature by the journalist's choice of verb to frame the utterance. Quirk and colleagues (1985: 1024) offer examples of **reporting verbs** that can be used in this way: say, explain, insist, remark, state, argue, warn, recall or declare. The shades of meaning we associate with such verbs can influence how we interpret even a direct quotation. For example, this appeared in a feature relating to an athlete preparing for the Olympic Games: "I'm a bit worried", she stutters. 'Here, the choice of *stutters* carries the connotation that the athlete lacks confidence in the context of the question and in delivering the quote. In a feature about vintage car renovation, the following: "'Not many of the American cars have many original parts left on them", explains my guide on arrival.' In this case, the choice of *explains* carries the implication that the writer was unaware of this potential problem and had to be enlightened, and also lends a mood of authority and truth to the quote itself.

Journalistic control over the utterance can also be exerted through the use of **free direct speech** without reporting clauses. In this way, the journalist is able to paraphrase part of the utterance, but leaves the reader to link this summary with the actual quoted utterance. For example, former Spice Girl Mel Brown was interviewed about her choice of names for her baby: 'Brown said she had thought hard about the child's names: "Angel, as she was my little angel through my pregnancy. Iris, as it's my grandma's name. Murphy, because he's the dad. And Brown, because I'm the mum!"' (*Closer*, 27 October 2007). In this way, the reader has to infer from the context who the speaker is, and thus the text requires greater reader engagement.

Greater journalistic control can be exercised through the use of **indirect speech**. This is where the thoughts or sayings are reported without quotation but with attribution to the speaker. For example, the direct quotation we saw above from the female athlete could be made into indirect speech to read: 'She told us she was a bit worried.' The process of converting from direct to indirect speech involves more than just removing the inverted commas to indicate speech. The addition of a **subordinating conjunction** ('she told us') is required to explicitly mark syntactic dependency, and thus anchoring the quotation within the feature. There is also a stylistic need to change from first person to third person, so here *I* becomes *she*. A further linguistic change is the backshift in the tense of the verb and time deictic, which reduces the immediacy of the utterance.

This use of indirect speech allows the journalist to gain more control over the utterance, both in terms of editing for length and style. Whilst the utterance may still be clearly attributed, looser connections are possible through this strategy and the paraphrasing can be more vague in its source. For example, 'Sources close to the prince have said he is looking forward to the challenges of his new role' removes the utterance from attribution to a specific individual and places it in the realm of shadowy anonymous groups of people. Sometimes, there is no reference to even a vague source, and the attribution is stated authoritatively as fact, for example, 'Most children have mobile phones'. Such unattributed sources are the least reliable and journalists generally try to avoid using them unless they fall within the 'common sense' discourse of their potential readers.

The linguistic choices made by the feature writer to strengthen the evidentiality of the piece and show the writer's viewpoint are reflected in the different ways of reporting this evidence to show distance from or alignment with the diverse sources of information. They may also be used to hide some sort of temporal disjuncture, such as an utterance which pre-dates the research for this feature by some time. Overall, we can represent the use of evidentiality in magazine features through the following chart (Table 3.3):

Table 3.3 The use of evidentiality in magazine features.

Most immediate	$\Rightarrow$	Least immediate
Direct speech	Free direct speech	Indirect speech

Coherence

Rather than just informing, a magazine feature will be expected to elaborate and explain: this is the 'in-depth' nature of a feature. The coherence of the feature refers to those rhetorical relations that describe not just what part of a feature is, but what it is doing. It is coherence that makes the text comprehensible, through the linking of arguments and statements. Referred to by Delin (2000) as 'discursivity', coherence relates to the underlying semantic unity by which the reader understands the text's propositions, actions or events to fit together. This is not something that exists in the grammatical structure of the text but in the understanding of language and context that people bring to the text with them. As George Yule explains:

It is people who 'make sense' of what they read and hear. They try to arrive at an interpretation that is in line with their experience of the way the world is. Indeed, our ability to make sense of what we read is probably only a small part of that general ability we have to make sense of what we perceive or experience in the world.

(Yule, 1996: 126)

An example of this reliance on the knowledge of readers to bring understanding to the text can be found in the standfirst to a feature about the wife of the founder of the mail-order business, Boden:

Sophie Boden talks about the highs and loves of married life with the man behind *that* catalogue. ('What it's like to be ... Mrs Boden', *Easy Living*, April 2005)

Here, the journalist relies on the reader to make the connection between the subject of the feature and the middle-class mail-order company, Boden. This is emphasized through the italicization of the determiner *that*, providing a chatty, gossipy tone to the feature as though it were one friend reporting a conversation with someone of mutual interest to another friend. Without the background knowledge that such a mail-order company exists, this would make little sense, but having this knowledge not only draws the reader into the article but also makes them feel part of a community in which such 'Boden Woman' is familiar.

Poorly written or edited features will have 'gaps' in them as those elements required for coherence are missing or are out of context. Examples of coherent elements to aid discursivity include:

Temporal sequences

Example. *When* Price returns from the school run, she starts to tidy the house ...

Contrasts

Example. *Although* she has access to a vast wardrobe, she tends to wear only a few key outfits.

Cause/result

Example. *After* a series of movie disasters, he returned to the stage.

Elaboration, describing an event/situation in more detail

Everett is comically glum about the sanitization of show business – the military schedules of early nights and abstinence enforced by po-faced publicists, and all the 'hollow, vulnerable' parties that made him long for Studio 54's carnival of freaks.
(adapted from Delin 2000: 108) (examples taken from *Guardian Weekend*, 29 September 2012)

These relationships of coherence hold the text together and provide the links through which readers can make sense of the article. So far, these principles of coherence could be applied to any text, and not just a magazine feature. However, they are of particular interest to us because where these links are absent, the reader is invited to assemble the text themselves as part of the pleasure of reading. An example of such an outward breakdown in coherence occurs in the following example, which is a feature about the wife of the founder of the Boden mail-order catalogue:

She's the backbone of the family, juggling the needs of three school-age daughters with supporting Johnnie and organising their busy lives in two homes, in London and Dorset. *And* she's learning French. 'We have a theory that you have work, home and a social life, but you can only really do two. So we choose work and home. Our social life is shot of pieces.'
(*Easy Living*, April 2005)

Outwardly, there is a lack of coherence between the elements in this extract, where the main elements relating to Sophie's role as home and family manager are disrupted in the middle by a the minor sentence '*And* she's learning French'. This does not fit with the rest of the feature, and the emphasis on the additive 'and' would imply that this is intended to be an elaboration that is noteworthy. However, as Grice (1975) points out, politeness proceeds on the understanding that particular 'maxims' will be maintained including quantity (which should be proportionate) and, in this case, relevance (see also Brown and Levinson, 1987). What may otherwise sit awkwardly and could leave the reader puzzling over the relevance of this seemingly unnecessary detail instead invites the reader to marvel at the diversity, and wonderful achievement of the feature's subject.

Also, coherence can be used in magazine features to engage readers in a sense of community by elliptical reference to previous issues of the publication, with the assumption that they are regular readers rather than a novice or mere occasional reader. In terms of the understandings required to engage in magazine discourse as a competent reader, it is important that the relevance of such forays would be clear to any practised reader.

Point-of-view

Part of the function of magazine features is that they convey an opinion rather than merely setting out facts. This is one of the main differences between newspaper journalism and magazine journalism. In the Introduction, we stated that language is inherently ideological and it is therefore inevitable that journalism is going to have elements of bias. However, with magazine features, the journalism is routinely emphatic in disavowing any sense of neutrality. This can often be identified through the use of the first person pronoun *I*, which, as we have already suggested in this chapter, is common in magazine features which can be written from the first person perspective.

Within magazine features, we also find a greater emphasis on the use of affective and experiential values. Affective meaning employs language which conveys a positive or negative evaluation on the part of the writer. This is often coupled with experiential values (Fairclough, 1989: 112), more often than not including the ideological or personal beliefs of the writer. As members of a discursive community, the readers are implicitly assumed to share in the writer's beliefs. Readers are led by the journalist's point-of-view into a preferred reading of the text. To return to the *Easy Living* feature on Sophie Boden, we can see here how the reader is invited to join in a positive assessment of the 'Boden Woman' figure:

'I don't feel I've got to be 'Boden Woman', but why would I spend good money on other clothes when it's all lovely? I'm going to make the most of it.' Sophie Boden's voice is muffled as she dives into her wardrobe to bring out another item from the eponymous clothing empire run by her husband. Who could argue, really? The Boden catalogue, ubiquitous in middle-class homes the country over, is full of what Mrs B calls 'clothes that cover you up, keep you warm and make you feel good about yourself.'

(*Easy Living*, April 2005)

The discursive community, as we saw in the editor's letter, is one in which there are shared values and points-of-view. In this feature, we can see a continuation of the gossipy, chatty tone, with the journalist and the interviewee apparently sitting in Sophie's bedroom going through her wardrobe. The free indirect speech of Sophie, promoting the clothing range ('why would I spend good money on other clothes?'), is followed up by the journalist with a question directed at the reader – 'who could argue, really' – invoking a sense of agreement and complicity. This sense of informal collusion is further enhanced by the use of the colloquial 'Mrs B' to refer to Sophie when quoting from her directly, as she continues her praise for her clothing range.

Conclusion

As we said at the introduction to this chapter, the craft of magazine journalism is writing on a specialized topic to an interested and specialized audience. Even where magazines are concerned with broader matters of popular culture and celebrity gossip, a sense of community of reading and common purpose is central to magazine writing. In this chapter we have tried to outline some of the ways we can look at this. We have concentrated on magazines for women, as these are more prevalent than those for men, yet use the same linguistic features to engage their readers. This is not the case in terms of content, as different magazines address quite divergent readers, assuming quite different sets of values and preferred styles of engagement. It will certainly be possible and interesting for readers to extend this analysis beyond gender, to examine magazines aimed at hobbyists, interest groups, political constituencies, and music and cultural consumers. Also, by mapping out the key factors of evidentiality, coherence and point-of-view, we have stressed the importance of seeing the underlying discourses of magazine coverage in terms different to those of most other forms of journalism; with a particular emphasis on personalization and subjective forms of writing, and how these operate to cultivate shared beliefs and values between journalists and readers.

Newspaper journalism

Introduction

In this chapter, we will be looking at the language of newspapers. We will reflect upon the structure of a news story, beginning with the essential role of the headline in drawing attention to and priming the story, before discussing the importance of news values and their emphasis. We will stress the role of news values as determining professional and compositional practice, looking at the example of celebrity coverage. Two matters the chapter will be particularly concerned with highlighting will be the distinctions in the use of language between 'quality' and 'popular' newspapers, looking at how the same story is covered across two different titles and the place of gender in newspaper discourse.

News values as everyday practice

The order of priorities, emphasis and manner of expression we find in a news story are determined by those 'news values' we looked at in the Introduction; that is, the criteria by which stories 'count' as news. In the Introduction, we first looked at a list of news values that incorporated the original list by Galtung and Ruge (1965) with recent additions by Bell (1991) and Harcup and O'Neill (2017).

As Stuart Allan (2010: 72) points out, these terms of selection draw upon the professional and lived environment of the journalist in a way that extends even beyond the stated criteria of 'cultural relevance'. This is important, since Hall and colleagues (1997: 54) remind us:

> Things are newsworthy because they represent the changefulness, the unpredictability and the conflictual nature of the world. But such events cannot be allowed to remain in the limbo of the 'random' they must be brought within the horizon of the 'meaningful'. This bringing of events within the realms of meaning means, in essence, referring unusual and unexpected events to the 'maps of meaning' which already form the basis of cultural knowledge, into which the social world is already 'mapped'.

These grammars of meaning and interpretation are not only social, however, but also form part of professional practice. In this way, and guided by the compositional requirements of that particular edition (Galtung and Ruge, 1965), we find newspapers routinely divided into specific sections dedicated to Home News, World News, Sport, Celebrity, Entertainment, Politics, Business, Health and Science, Lifestyle and Fashion, and so on. On the larger papers, each section will have a dedicated reporter who specializes in that area, although often the same journalists will be asked to produce copy across a number of sections, employing appropriately variant styles.

Occasionally, a story will also appear in the same newspaper in different sections, as its potential for engaging different news values is such that it may be deemed to merit separate coverage. For example, the England men's football team playing an international match will appear in the Sports section, but also may appear on the front page as 'home news' if there is some element such as unexpectedness or negativity that propels it into the realm of domestic or international news. Similarly, an oil spill in the Gulf of Mexico in the summer of 2010 was reported in the 'business section' in relation to the financial implications for the future of BP's shares, but also appeared in the 'science' section of many papers in reports about the environmental damage of the oil spill, highlighting negativity, unexpectedness and superlativity ('the biggest oil spill in US history'). Indeed, the story also reached the front pages when the US president got involved and was perceived as drawing on anti-British discourses, which took on news values of negativity, unexpectedness and, most relevant for many right-wing British newspapers, proximity, with the perceived attack on Britain and Britishness being articulated.

As Harcup (2009: 48) points out, knowing how to apply news values appropriately is a key professional skill of the journalist. The manner in which these values are expressed offers an insight not only into the dominant social mores at any given moment in time, but also in the priorities of the news room.

Headlines

So once a story is selected for inclusion, how should we set about understanding its composition? As we found in the previous chapter's section on magazine covers, the headline in a newspaper is the hook that attracts readers to pick up the paper or pause at that page. On national papers particularly, headlines are usually written by the subeditor, not the journalist whose story it accompanies. The subeditor is skilled in using language to attract attention to a story, often sharing the motives of advertising to amuse and beguile the reader. One specific feature of newspaper headlines, though, is the fact that the conventions of page layout demand that headlines to be in a large, eye-catching font. Because of this, there are space constraints that mean news headlines tend to employ words of seven letters or fewer. This leads to a special 'news headline register', where certain longer words and phrases are lexicalized in shorter words which are rarely used outside of this genre. These are often chosen by subeditors for their emotive, playful or informal connotations. For example, in British newspapers, verbs such as the process of telling some off or reprimanding them is relexicalized as 'rap'. To criticize strongly is to 'blast' or 'slam', and to investigate is to 'probe'. Nouns can be relexicalized too, such as where young children become 'tots', and academics or scientists become 'boffins' and, sometimes, 'gurus'.

Another feature of headlines is the adoption of advertising wordplay such as the use of puns. As Martin Conboy (2006: 19) has suggested, wordplay in British tabloid newspapers can 'often precede the strict news agenda if a good pun is as good if not better than a good storyline'. This eagerness to have fun with language is not exclusively a feature of tabloid newspapers (the popular papers we will be looking more closely later), but the accompanying irreverence and ridicule is rarely found in broadsheet newspapers. This word-play is not, however, straightforward. Some puns work on the basis of some words sounding identical, but carrying a different meaning and often a different spelling: these are **homophonic puns**. For example, the free newspaper, *Metro*, found humour in the then British Prime Minister Theresa May's failure to gain an acceptable deal with the European Union (EU) with the headline: 'Stuck in the muddle with EU' (26 March 2019). This headline employs the straightforward homophonic pun on EU/you, and the partial homophonic pun of muddle/middle. Superficially, this works as a description of May's impossible position of negotiating between the EU and the UK parliament, but is elevated to greater humour through the **intertextual** reference to the 1973 song, 'Stuck in the Middle with You' by Stealers Wheel. Thus the pun works as a homophonic metaphor as well as intertexual reference, both elements adding up to create a humorous headline. This is both a visual pun, and semantic reference, so works on oth visual and oral levels.

A more complex example which only works in the written form comes from the Scottish edition of *The Sun* that used the headline 'Wendy's Talking Sheet' over an update on a controversy over party donations, in which aides of Scottish politician Wendy Alexander had distributed a 'crib sheet' to keep colleagues on message. 'Wendy's Talking Sheet' draws upon an ambivalent use of an apostrophe (from abbreviation to possessive) and plays on the similarity of the sounds of 'sheet' and 'shite', particularly when spoken with a marked Scottish accent.

Another frequent sort of pun is the **homonymic pun**, where words which sound similar and are spelled the same, but carry different and not necessarily related meanings. For example, in a story about a burglar who had been apprehended by a Polish homeowner, the headline was 'Pole Axed' (*Daily Mirror*, 29 June 2010), which draws on the literal meaning of Pole meaning Polish, but also the metaphorical meaning of stopping violently ('pole-axed'). It is the same word, but carries a different meaning and therefore an opportunity to fashion a pun.

Another technique often used in headlines is to use **partial puns**. For example, a story in *The Sun* about the amount of money being spent on temporary consultants by the government ran with the headline 'Dosh and Go'. The partial pun on dosh/wash which carries a colloquial term for money that links with the informality of the newspaper's editorial style. This headline also evokes a well-known phrase used as the trademark of a brand of shampoo and conditioner indicating speed and convenience – *Wash and Go* – but in a manner in which the convenience is purposively informalized by the inclusion of the punning 'dosh'. The headline therefore primes a set of assumptions about the lack of care exercised in government expenditure, linking spending with assumptions over common and everyday greed. This use of puns is frequently found in tabloids, which Conboy (2006: 23) suggests politicizes journalistic language by directing popular forms of engagement at the institutions and personnel of power, and toying with the very lexicon of instrumental government.

Such a pun on a well-known phrase is an example of **intertextuality**. Intertextuality relies on a reader and writer sharing background knowledge of a phrase's or text's original or earlier use, and carrying this knowledge into the current use. We saw elements of this in the *Wash and Go* example above. Another example of this occurs in the well-known *Sun* headline (10 April 2009) which ran above a story about a senior police officer, Bob Quick, resigning within hours of being photographed carrying secret documents into Downing Street, inadvertently revealing plans for an anti-terrorism raid. *The Sun*'s subeditors seized on the police officer's unusual name in their headline: 'You can't quit quicker than a thick Quick quitter'. In the British context, this tongue-twister headline carries the same rhythm and linguistic play as a well-known jingle for a car maintenance garage, Kwik-Fit, which runs 'You can't fit quicker than a Kwik-Fit fitter'. In *The Sun*'s clever wordplay, the partial puns serve to highlight this link with the original jingle whilst also passing judgement on the inept police officer, even if the adjective 'thick' carries the unlikely connotations of stupidity rather than the more obvious carelessness of the action. This intertextuality requires the very active involvement of a newspaper's readers, something that John Storey (1997: 130–4) argues is characteristic of the **carnivalesque** nature of popular culture throughout history, where the powerless temporarily enjoy expressive prominence in poking fun at the mighty.

Aside from often-entertaining wordplays in news headlines, there are also specific grammatical choices that are part of the headline register. These often feature the reduction of function words (such as determiners, auxiliary verbs, pronouns). Most commonly, headlines comprise noun phrases, dictated by the use of a **headword**. A headword (Graddol et al., 1994: 80) determines the syntactic type of a phrase, and is the main focus of a phrase. For example, 'Cancer op tot goes home', contains the headword 'tot' (noting the journalese use of tot instead of young child) which is premodified by 'cancer op' to produce a **noun phrase**. To identify the headword, adjectives can be removed and the utterance still 'makes sense', although in this case the news-worthy circumstances of the tot would be lost. We can also see that this sentence is not grammatically complete; it lacks determiners such as '*this* tot' or '*that* tot'. To write this out in grammatically complete English, the headline would read something along the lines of 'A young child who has had surgery for cancer goes home' (the phrase 'goes home' is also a colloquial rendering of the longer phrase 'is released from hospital after treatment'). Here, we have added a determiner 'a' and added tense with the auxiliary verbs 'has had', whilst also altering the syntax, primarily to avoid adjectival premodification. As we can see, the original headline is much shorter, yet still provides a clear indication of the associated story – to the seasoned headline reader, that is.

We have just commented on the importance of attaching adjectives to noun-phrases, without which the tot's situation would have been unclear. But it is worth saying a little more on the importance of such descriptions in headlines, particularly in how the processes of distillation of meaning they embody can reduce the nuance of a story. The reduction of words in a headline can lead to a noun phrase, distant from the interpretative subtleties of spoken language and heavy in judgement. For example, 'Thigh-Flashing Esther and the Battle of the Downing St Catwalk' was the headline to the *Daily Mail* report about a government reshuffle (16 July 2014), accompanied by a full-length photo of politician Esther McVey walking in a tailored dress. Here, the noun 'Esther' is premodified with a hyphenated adjective. Here, where the noun phrase comprised the entire headline, the series of sexualizing adjectives amplify the mood of evaluation of the female politicians that the story went on to develop.

The sexism underpinning this article provoked a great deal of media comment, such as *The Guardian* headline (16 July 2014): 'Daily Mail goes back in time to analyse female MPs as sex objects.' Here, the noun phrase 'Thigh-flashing Esther' is replaced by 'female MPs' in a more neutral way, their gender being relevant only in response to the sexualization of only the female politicians in the *Mail*'s article.

The production of pithy and attractive headlines is one of the key skills of a subeditor. There is, as any newspaper editor will attest, an 'art' to writing the headline: it is the headline that gets the readers' attention and pulls them into the story. We have pointed out how the strategies of headline production engage the seasoned newspaper reader in an intertextual game, where popular cultural tropes can be used to situate a story within an immediately recognizable cultural context, and prick the pretences of power. Yet, dangers lurk. Cutting through the nuances of a story has the potential to reduce its meaning to accord with our basest prejudices. In headline speak: 'journos beware'.

The structure of news stories

Just as there are conventions we associate with the news headline, so we find corresponding conventions in newspaper stories. According to Labov and Walesky (1967) and Labov (1972), in our use of oral narratives in everyday language, we routinely follow the same basic structure. This comprises six elements:

1. Abstract – a summary of what the story is going to be about.
2. Orientation – who is involved, where, when?
3. Complicating action – what happened next? And then?
4. Evaluation – So what was this about?
5. Resolution – how the story concluded?
6. Coda – that's it, story over.

These elements are largely chronological, and usually appear in this order. As Barthes (1970) points out, such oral narratives contain an element of suspense, which he refers to as 'hermeneutic codes': that element of any narrative that remains ambiguous and is held back from the reader under a point of resolution ('the diegetic truth', in Barthes's terms).

If we take an example of a news story, we can begin to explore the ways in which such stories are structured, and how they differ from oral narratives. If we look in detail at a story that appeared in the *Daily Mail* on 9 June 2010 and featured the pop singer Kylie Minogue, we can begin by examining the chronological structure of the story.

JUST PEACHY

Kylie Minogue is a gem in her plunging coral dress at jewellery bash – but only just avoids getting her heels caught

By *Daily Mail* reporter
9th June 2010

1. She only turned 42 less than two weeks ago, but Kylie Minogue managed to pull off a youthful look as she attended a London party last night.
2. Fresh from her recent trip to New York, the pop star looked stunning in her over-length, coral, slashed-to-thigh BodyAmr dress with plunging neckline.
3. However, she flirted the disaster in a pair of YSL golden platforms, treading on the gown more than once and nearly getting caught up in it.
4. Despite being well-known for being a diminutive 5 ft 1, the long dress and towering Yves Saint Laurent platforms gave Minogue the illusion of being much taller.
5. The Australian was the guest of honour at the Tous jewellery store party at their Regent Street branch last night.
6. She made sure she proved a worthy ambassador for the brand as she wore a large gold ring, bracelet and heavy earrings.
7. Minogue has been modelling for Tous for three years and has appeared in several international advertising campaigns for the firm.
8. Last week, the Locomotion star travelled to New York to promote her new album Aphrodite.
9. As well as appearing on several U.S. talk shows, she also performed a gay nightclub Splash with hunky underwear-clad male dancers.
10. On Wednesday, she hosted the inaugural amfAR New York Inspiration Gala, at The New York Public Library to honour her designer pal Jean Paul Gaultier for his contribution to fashion and his fundraising efforts for AIDS charities.

11. Minogue recently denied rumours she was suffering difficulties with her boyfriend of 18 months, Spanish model Andres Velencoso, 32.
12. Writing on her Twitter page recently, Minogue said: 'Wowza … love life rumours have gone mad.'
13. 'Please pay no attention peeps. My birthday was magical with AV (Velencoso) and friends.'

It is possible to see here how the chronology of this story operates:

1. Kylie has been modelling jewellery for Tous for three years.
2. Kylie celebrated her forty-second birthday two weeks ago.
3. Kylie recently used Twitter to deny rumours of problems with her boyfriend.
4. Kylie went to New York last week to promote her latest album.
5. Kylie appeared on several US chat shows and performed at a gay nightclub whilst in New York.
6. Kylie hosted a fund-raising gala last Wednesday.
7. Kylie went to a party last night.
8. Kylie wore a long dress and jewellery by the party's sponsor.
9. Kylie didn't trip over her dress.

We can thus see that the news story does not follow a chronological sequence. The events underlying the story are not described in the order in which they unfold. Judy Delin (2000: 18) argues that this characteristic of a newspaper story, and directs us instead to a structure that comprises three main elements:

1. Headline (Just Peachy)
2. Lead paragraph (Kylie Minogue is a gem …)
3. Body (paragraphs 1–13)

As we can see in this story, the **headline** draws attention to Kylie's dress and the problems she experiences in wearing this whilst attending a specific party. The **lead paragraph** compresses events and represents these as being 'newsworthy' in terms of offering an insight into the relationship between her age and physical attractiveness. The **body** of the story then expands with a detailed description of her outfit and its relevance to the event she is attending, intermingled with paragraphs relating to her recent trip to the United States. Finally, the story ends with a quotation from Kylie's Twitter page refuting rumours (repeated in this story) that she was having problems with her boyfriend. We can see that, whilst the headline focuses on Kylie's outfit, and the accompanying picture shows her arriving at the party and smiling for photographers, most of the story is directed towards previous events, particularly her trip to the United States.

Following this, the body of the news story can contain a range of perspectives, comments and background details. Who gets to have their comments heard and who doesn't, or whose comments are paraphrased is something we looked at in the chapter on magazine features. The use of quotations to support a story relates to the journalist's need to provide the story with 'authority'. In this story centred around Kylie Minogue, we can see only one quotation and that is from Kylie herself, via Twitter, and does not relate to the main story as in the headline. However, the relevance of this quotation is part of the intrinsic interest of the story: that a 42-year-old woman is able to 'pull off a youthful look', and has had a boyfriend who is ten years younger than her for the last eighteen months.

The relevance of quotations to a news story is similar to that of a magazine feature (we see this in the chapter on magazines). The difference between a newspaper and a magazine is most often found in the recency of the story in the newspaper. Often published on a daily basis, stories in newspapers are expected to emphasize their currency (weekly papers are less obliged to do so). In the rush to get a story to print, the journalist may often need to furnish it with quotations from less recent sources. Whilst this may not be identified explicitly in the text, linguistically we can spot such quotations by the grammatical construction with allows for such a sleight of hand. For example, an indirect quotation that is framed using the past participle can indicate that it is from a much older source, for example, 'She has spoken of her illness ...' rather than 'She spoke of her illness ...', which implies a close chronological connection.

If we look at again that the Kylie Minogue story, we can see that it carries a feature of newspaper stories in its repetition of events. Her trip to New York is mentioned in paragraphs 2, 8, 9 and 10, whilst her appearance at the London party occurs in paragraphs 1, 2, 3, 4, 5, 6 and 7. The more consecutive thread relates to the main story, with the less recent story of her New York trip circling around this. This is typical of news stories, according to Alan

Bell (1991: 99), even though 'disrupting narrative chronology is cognitively confusing'. He goes on to comment:

> The story cycles around the action, returning for more detail on each circuit, and interspersing background and other events. The technique moves like a downward spiral through the available information. This is, in fact, described by journalists as the 'inverted pyramid' style – gathering all the main points at the beginning and progressing through decreasingly important information.
>
> (Bell, 1991: 168)

What has become known as this 'inverted pyramid' structure of print news stories places the Labov's 'abstract' first, as this contains the most important elements of the story. These elements are themselves determined by how news values are applied within the story, what is regarded as newsworthy in one newspaper may be considered differently in others. Why, for example, might the UK tabloid the *Daily Mail* feature prominently a story of a pop star's outfit worn at a party, whilst the story does not appear at all in the same day's edition of the broadsheet, *The Guardian*? Also, that Kylie had been taking part in an event that was part of London's 'Jewellery Week' is not mentioned in the *Daily Mail* article, but a story relating to this event does appear in the 'Business' pages of *The Guardian*. Here, the news values of the story are largely what are used to judge its appropriateness and worthiness for coverage.

Popular and quality styles

Of course, some students of journalism might suggest that pop stars such as Kylie should not be featured in newspapers in the first place. Certainly, the emphasis on 'celebrity' differs from one paper to the next. Across a number of national contexts, newspapers are divided into occasionally problematic categories of the quality and the popular press. A substantial amount of work has been conducted on the cultural differences between these two categories (Tulloch and Sparks, 2000). Of course, one objection is that the opposition plays out a hierarchy of judgement already established in the definition of one category as the bearers of a certain 'quality' absent, by implication, from their more 'popular' competitors (Temple, 2008). One way of thinking about the difference in practical terms is in the level of political engagement. The political coverage in the popular press is less in both quantity and depth than their 'quality' press counterparts.

On the other hand, looking at the normative terms of this popular/quality distinction critically, another approach has been to see them as engaged in different sorts of discursive activity: related in terms of their commitment to the norms of journalism, but manifesting divergent priorities and offering different forms of appeal to their readership. Higgins (2010), for example, writes about how newspapers in the British context have come to represent various social groupings and interests, along the axes of social class, politics, gender and lifestyle.

It is the British context, and its sharp division between quality and popular (or 'tabloid' press) we are going to look at here; examining how two different newspapers deal with the same set of events. The context of the story in question is a British politician who had announced his divorce. This first extract (Table 4.1) is the report from the 'quality' broadsheet newspaper *The Guardian*:

Table 4.1 *The Guardian*, 7 September 2018.

1. **Boris Johnson and Marina Wheeler announce divorce**
2. Former foreign secretary and senior lawyer make statement after reports of unfaithfulness
   Staff and agencies
3. Fri 7 Sep 2018 09.55 BST
   Boris Johnson and his wife, Marina Wheeler, have announced that they are in the process of a divorce after separating some time ago.
4. The former foreign secretary and the senior lawyer, both 54, have been married for 25 years. They made the announcement in a joint statement after a story appeared in the Sun on Friday detailing claims that Johnson was unfaithful.
5. Johnson resigned as foreign secretary in July over his opposition to Theresa May's Chequers Brexit plan. He has since written a series of articles criticising the government, which have been viewed as attempts to position himself as an alternative prime minister.
6. Wheeler is a human rights lawyer who became a Queen's Counsel in 2016. Johnson credited her as a key voice in his decision to support Brexit before the referendum.
7. In a joint personal statement issued to the Press Association through a family friend, Johnson and Wheeler said: 'Several months ago, after 25 years of marriage, we decided it was in our best interests to separate.'
8. 'We have subsequently agreed to divorce and that process is under way. As friends we will continue to support our four children in the years ahead. We will not be commenting further.'

As we noted in the last section, the most important part of a newspaper story is the opening paragraph, and this one does a considerable amount of work. First of all, the opening offers a partial summary of the developments that led to this point, where the politician's name is immediately followed by a subordinate clause to give his wife's name to remind the reader of her role ('Boris Johnson and his wife, Marina Wheeler' – paragraph 4). The human element of the story is emphasized at this early stage, both in terms of the professional status of one of the main agents ('former foreign secretary and the senior lawyer' – paragraph 5), with their ages and length of marriage.

Something that is notable in this story is the ordering and distribution of the additional details. In keeping with the loading of information and newsworthy characteristics in the opening paragraph, it is clear that the details become more adorned as the text of the story proceeds. In *The Guardian* version, the details therefore become more expansive as the story proceeds. We learn that it is a collaborative announcement in paragraph 5 ('They made the announcement in a joint statement'), but that this was prompted by a story in another newspaper relating to Johnson's extramarital affair, glossed here as 'unfaithful'.

We learn more of Johnson's role as politician in the next paragraph (6), which finishes with speculation as to his future: 'attempts to position himself as an alternative prime minister'. This biographical information is balanced by details of Wheeler's career in the following paragraph (7), where the attribution of her as a 'senior lawyer' in paragraph 5 is expanded to include her specialism ('human rights'), her seniority ('a Queen's Counsel') and then something of her political views in crediting her with influencing Johnson to support Brexit in 2016.

The story finishes with a longer quotation from the joint statement, with reference to its release through the Press Association via an anonymous 'family friend'. There are no other personal details beyond the mention of 'our four children' in the final line of the quoted statement. Throughout, the two main players are presented through their surnames or job titles after the first paragraph where they are named in full.

This story explicitly features the couple's joint statement, but hints that this is something that only appeared after intimate details of their marital problems emerged in the popular tabloid newspaper *The Sun*. If we turn to this newspaper's coverage of the same press release (Figure 4.1), we can see some of the differences in the ways 'quality' and 'redtop tabloid' newspapers use language in their reporting.

There are a number of key differences between the treatment of the story in *The Sun* and in *The Guardian*. The most superficial difference is in the number

Figure 4.1 The Sun. 2 September 2018.

of words devoted to the story: in its full form, *The Guardian* story is two-thirds the length of *The Sun*'s. Yet despite this difference in length, the descriptive language used by *The Sun* is substantially more expansive (Table 4.2).

The Sun's expressive register finds form in the references to Boris Johnson. Within the classic tabloid lexicon, where sexual excesses are referred to using the

Table 4.2

1. BOJO DIVORCE
2. Bonking Boris Booted Out By Wife
3. Top Tory accused of cheating on her again
4. Couple separated after she had enough
Breaking
By Neal Baker
7th September 2018, 9:46 am
5. **BORIS Johnson and long-suffering wife Marina Wheeler are divorcing.**
6. In a joint statement the pair said they separated 'some time ago' and are now in the process of getting a divorce.
7. Boris Johnson and his high-flying lawyer wife, both 54, are now living apart and no longer socialise together
8. It comes after The Sun exclusively revealed the couple, both 54, were living apart.
9. The short statement read: 'Several months ago, after 25 years of marriage, we decided it was in our best interests to separate.'
10. 'We have subsequently agreed to divorce and that process is under way.'
11. 'As friends we will continue to support our four children in the years ahead. We will not be commenting further.'
12. Earlier this year, rumours had circulated in Westminster that Boris had started to give his police protection officers the slip for illicit liaisons while he was Foreign Secretary.
13. Boris pictured cycling around Westminster this morning just hours before the divorce announcement.
14. Boris had been accused of cheating again on lawyer Marina — who married in 1993.
15. The former Foreign Secretary had fathered a child in 2009 with arts consultant Helen Macintyre.
16. And in 2004 Bojo admitted having an affair with the writer Petronella Wyatt who fell pregnant and had an abortion.
17. Boris had initially denied the affair — famously dubbing it an 'inverted pyramid of piffle' — but was sacked from the shadow cabinet for lying to then-Tory leader Michael Howard.
18. But both times Marina — mum to Lara, 25, Milo Arthur, 23, Cassia Peaches, 21, and Theodore Apollo, 19 — eventually took him back.
19. Fashion journalist Lara is understood to have been overheard exploding with rage at her philandering dad.
20. She is said to have told pals at a party he 'is a selfish bastard'.
21. And she insisted to one friend: 'Mum is finished with him. She will never take him back now.'

verb 'bonking' (Spiegl, 1989: 75) is here expanded alliteratively in the headline to 'Bonking Boris'. The front-page headline (Figure 4.1) is highly alliterative in full: 'Bonking Boris Booted Out By Wife.' This passive construction, with the actor ('wife') placed at the end of the headline, is found elsewhere in this article (Table 4.2), with Johnson placed as the passive object. For example, in the sub headline: 'Top Tory accused of cheating on her again' (paragraph 3). By this strategy, we can see Johnson himself is placed at the beginning of the sentence, and is thus its focus. In other examples, we find Johnson and Wheeler acting together, as with *The Guardian* report, when citing their joint statement: 'Boris Johnson and long-suffering wife Marina Wheeler are divorcing' (paragraph 5); 'Boris Johnson and his high-flying lawyer wife, both 54, are now living apart' (paragraph 7).

As with *The Guardian* report, Johnson is referred to as 'former foreign secretary' (paragraph 15), but there are only two occasions on which he is referred to by his full name (paragraph 5 and 7). Unlike *The Guardian* examples, it is not his surname that is used elsewhere. Most frequently, it is his first name, with 'Boris' appearing four times (paragraphs 12, 14 and 17, plus picture caption in paragraph 13). This draws a sense of familiarity with the politician that is enhanced by the more creative use of a collocation of the first phonemes of his first name and surname: 'Bojo' (paragraphs 1 and 16).

The adjectival descriptions of the two main players in this report are also worth exploring. As with *The Guardian* report, Wheeler is given her professional occupation of lawyer, but this is rearticulated as 'high flying' rather than *The Guardian*'s 'senior', rendering it more colloquial. There is no mention of her professional standing or her political influence. Instead, there is a focus on her personal life, as we find the opening sentence referring to her as 'long-suffering wife'(paragraph 5) and later post-modified in a subordinate clause as 'mum to Lara' (paragraph 18). In a quotation from Lara, she is named as 'mum' (paragraph 21). This contrasts with the framing of this quotation by *The Sun*, where Johnson is named 'philandering dad' (paragraph 19), and then in a quotation from Lara, 'selfish bastard' (paragraph 20).

The naming practices in *The Sun* – themselves essential to specify the roles of each actor in the story – are employed to add detail and colour to the profile of the allegedly guilty party. In this way, Wheeler is framed less in terms of her professional and political identify as she was in *The Guardian*, than as a wronged-against wife and mother. She is ultimately being domesticated (a point we will return to shortly), which is set against the way Johnson's identity is framed, as we shall see.

This adds to the detail that comes in the report about Johnson's previous extramarital affairs. This is initially marked in the subheading (paragraph 3) 'Top Tory accused of cheating on her again'. Here, there is an **implicature** carried by 'again'. Implicatures are linguistic features that convey an additional meaning: in this case, it is that this is not the first time Johnson has had an extramarital affair. This is variously referred to as 'cheating' (paragraphs 3 and 14) and 'illicit liaisons' (paragraph 12) and 'affairs' (paragraphs 16 and 17). The subterfuge of his behaviour is enhanced by the report drawing on gossip that Johnson 'had started to give his police protection officers the slip for illicit liaisons while he was Foreign Secretary' (paragraph 12). This juxtaposes the senior political office of Foreign Secretary with the dishonest behaviour of Johnson in 'giving the slip' to his protection officers in order to engage in an extramarital affair. The picture that illustrates the story at this point is of Johnson cycling in Central London, captioned to contextualize it to a photo taken 'just hours before the divorce announcement' (paragraph 13), thus once again emphasizing Johnson's apparent lack of gravitas. The report then reminds the reader that Johnson and Wheeler had married in 1993 (paragraph 14), the reason for this explicit reference becoming clear when in the next two paragraphs there is support for the lack of moral gravitas with reference to previous examples of Johnson's extramarital affairs, implicit in the reference to 'fathering a child in 2009 with arts consultant Helen Macintyre' (paragraph 15), and 'in 2004 Bojo admitted having an affair with the writer Petronella Wyatt' (paragraph 16). There is additional information here, in that Wyatt 'fell pregnant and had an abortion'. In contrast with the affair with Macintyre, Johnson, linguistically at least, plays no part in the conception of the child, which serves to enhance the sense of a lack of commitment in his relationships. The only other mention of politics in this story comes at this point (paragraph 17), with the report repeating the story of Johnson's denial of his affair with Wyatt when challenged about this by his then party leader. That this was revealed to be a lie that led to his sacking is also repeated to develop further the picture of Johnson as an unreliable adulterer. Interesting in terms of newspaper language, at that point Johnson largely blamed the media for creating false stories. The illustrative quotation that is used in *The Sun* refers back to our earlier point about news stories appearing in an inverted pyramid. Here, Johnson is creatively using alliteration to emphasize his denial: 'an inverted pyramid of piffle'.

In discussing the differences in popular and quality newspaper style, Bell (1991: 105) offers the general observation that news styles are adapted to the anticipated audience, in a manner analogous to a 'speaker shifting her style to be more like the person she is talking to'. It is certainly true that papers in the quality category draw upon a quite focused lexicon and grammatical style. But there is much more to the difference than this, since popular newspapers draw upon their own lexicon and style, associated with and peculiar to popular journalism. Using their own conventions of language, popular papers are more inclined to write in order to engage the passions of their readership. As van Dijk (1988: 123) points out, news values are emphasized on the basis of their likely relevance to the reader (consonance), with a preference often given to instances of 'deviance and negativity'. Where such news values are present, negatively charged words such as 'bonking' can be used to emphasize the preferred mood of the story, and generate and hold out the offer to the readers to participate in a play of emotional exchange. This, in *The Sun* version of the story, is enhanced by the adjectival descriptions of the two main players which implies blame on one party more than the other.

Gender

In the previous chapter, we started to look at how communities of readers are created through gender in magazines. We will now take this opportunity to look at gender in newspapers, how newspaper content is geared towards specific genders and what this means.

Since Second-Wave Feminism in the 1960s and 1970s raised awareness of gender inequalities, there has been a great deal of research carried out into how women are disadvantaged in media coverage of them. Since theorists such as Dale Spender revealed English as an inherently sexist language, Second-Wave Feminism sought to raise awareness of this and eventually the

National Union of Journalists (NUJ) produced guidelines that encouraged journalists to think more about the language they used. The main elements of this are summarized in Table 4.3 below, which is taken from the NUJ's guidelines:

Table 4.3 National Union of Journalists good practice guidance for journailsts (adapted).

Dispreferred	Preferred
Businessman	Business manager, executive, business people
Newsman	Journalist
Cameraman	Camera operator, photographer
Dustman	Refuse collector
Policeman	Police officer
Salesman	Sales staff, shop worker
Stewards/air hostess	Flight attendant
Chairman	Chairperson, chairwoman, chair
Housewife	Shopper, consumer, cook
Authoress	Author – avoid -*ess* where possible
Mothers	(when we mean parents)
Girls (when over 18)	Women (especially in sports reporting)
Ladies, Mrs Mopp, dolls	Women – these, and puns arising from them are not funny.
Serviceman	Armed service personnel
Male nurse/woman doctor	Nurse, doctor

Many of these lexical items reflect changes in society that have led to wider employment opportunities for women, so now professions such as media production and business management are not exclusively male domains. Other terms relate to the assumption about female roles, such as childcare and domestic work. Newspaper style guides will indicate to journalists what the preferred lexical choice will be for that paper (such as *The Guardian*'s guide which tells its journalists to use 'actor' instead of 'actress' when referring to female actors), but there is also the case of the personal choice of title being used by the person who is being reported. We can see how this might be problematic in one report by the right-wing newspaper the *Daily Mail* (5 January 2007), concerning women being obstructed in their business careers by workplace strategies to discourage maternity leave and flexible working hours. 'Bosses "block women who want a career and a family"'. Within the article, two principal players are quoted: Jenny Watson 'chairman of the EOC' and Lorely Burt, who is referred to as the 'Liberal Democrat Women and Equality Spokesman'. In both cases, the women are given male-specific titles (chairman and spokesman), yet their personal preferences as shown in their respective websites was for 'chair' (in the case of Watson) and 'spokesperson' (for Burt). Thus we can see that, despite NUJ guidelines and the expressed preferences of the women concerned, there is a problematic use of gender-specific language being used by the journalist. It is all the more ironic that this is a report about gender equality in the workplace.

If we return briefly to the story about Kylie Minogue attending a party, we can begin to see how different genders are reported in the media and how this goes beyond the level of lexical choice that appears to be the main concern of the NUJ's guidelines. On a basic level, the story is based around Kylie's clothes and does not mention the reason why she was attending the party. Instead, this is used as a vehicle to comment about her age and her personal life. The relationship between this and gender stereotyping can be clearly articulated in Table 4.4 we used in the Magazine Journalism chapter, repeated more briefly as follows:

Table 4.4 Gender stereotypes

Men	Women
Power	Grace
Strength	Elegance
Independence	Dependence
Public life	Private life

As we can see, this also links with the lexical items we looked at briefly above, where the language of public work is closely aligned to masculinity. The report about Kylie Minogue is also placing her firmly in the realms of a story based around elegance and her private life: the only quotations in this story relate to her boyfriend. Kylie's professional status is acknowledged in relation to the release of her latest album, but this is framed within descriptions of a party-going, heterosexual lifestyle.

We shall return to the concept of 'clickbait' in more detail in Chapter 6, but if we look briefly at the ways in which the online version of the *Daily Mail* attracts readers' attention through its 'side bar of shame', we can see the verb and adjectives attached to photos of women reflect the idea of women being sexualized.

Women are frequently described as 'flaunting' their bodies, such as 'Mel C *flaunts* her incredible abs' and 'Kim Kardashian *flaunts* her hourglass figure'. If not flaunting, they may be 'displaying', such as 'Kayleigh Morris *displays* her incredible bikini body' and 'Marnie Simpson *displays* her blossoming baby bump'. Other verbs that carry connotations of deliberate exhibitionism include 'shows' (as in 'Lindsay Lohan *shows* plenty of cleavage') and, of course, exhibiting, for example 'Ashley Graham *exhibits* her jaw-dropping curves'. It should be noted that it is consistently the exhibiting of the body that is being described, and most frequently it is the fragmentation of the body into breasts (where 'busty' or 'cleavage' are the most common collocations) or legs (where 'pins' is the most frequently used noun). In this way, women's bodies are being commented as being willingly presented to us for scrutiny by the women themselves.

To illustrate this further, we will now look at the print media's representation of women who have appeared in the public eye more frequently as a result of policies to engage more women in public roles in the media. For example, in 2018 in Britain, the host of the most popular breakfast radio show, Chris Evans, announced he was leaving. The rumoured shortlist to replace him appeared to include only female broadcasters including Zoe Ball. We will look at one report of this story, appearing in the Scottish newspaper, *The Herald*, written by journalist Brian Beacom (Table 4.5).

Beacom starts with a pun on Ball's name, which draws readers into the article. He then uses conversational strategies such as the question 'Why?' to further include the reader. In common with several (mostly but not exclusively male) journalists, attempts to promote gender equality are regarded as being invalid. Beacom uses various strategies to demean Ball's worthiness.

Table 4.5 *The Herald*, 20 September 2018.

20th September, 2018
BBC's obsession with female presenters will backfire
Brian Beacom
Senior Features Writer, The Herald
14/2/16Â PA File Photo of Zoe Ball attending the EE Br

1. TIME to give Zoe Ball a little kicking. Why? The TV and radio presenter looks not only a shoo-in for the breakfast show slot on Radio 2, it's been claimed she was one of five female favourites for the job.
2. If you're a man hoping for radio's most prestigious slot, the only chance is to transgender and hope the oestrogen pills kick in before Chris Evans sets off to become a reborn Virgin.
3. The BBC, in its infinite wisdom, (i.e. director-general Tony Hall, who has pledged that half of BBC presenters will be women by 2020), looks to be following the road to gender equality so prescriptively it's making a mockery of the entire concept of meritocracy.
4. Now, this is not a representational petted lip on behalf of half the population; it's anger following on from frustration, wondering when will it stop.
5. Zoe Ball isn't a bad presenter, her Saturday afternoon show hold its own in terms of listeners, but it's an exercise in shallow cheeriness. The simile it suggests is of meeting someone at a party for the first time, who squeals with delight as she air kisses you twice – and then disappears to be someone else's best friend.
6. The breakfast show, however, demands more. Wogan was witty, irreverent and clever. Evans was big, loud and inventive. But there is little doubt that criteria has been ditched. There is little doubt Ball's hitting the back of the net is a result of the very loud demands of the Sound Women pressure group over a five-year period, set up to help women progress in radio.
7. Now, that intent is sound; yes, push women in broadcasting to succeed. But to not consider a male appointment is risible, given the likelihood there are some good young men out there.

We should begin by noting that, while this story concerns the vacancy of a high profile radio presenting job, it deals with gender and the domestic domain in connection with the possible replacement, Zoe Ball.

Table 4.6

Zoe Ball	Chris Evans
TV and radio presenter	Reborn Virgin
Ladette	Prankish, impish
Mother of two	

From this list, we can see that Ball is given her professional role, but is also subject to gendered stereotyping that contrasts her 'ladette' persona with that of the 'mother'. Ball was well known in the 1990s as being part of the ladette culture which saw young women behave in much the same way as young men, or 'lads', in terms of drinking, smoking and sexual permisssiveness. However, when this is applied to Ball, it is done in a disapproving way. For example (Table 4.7):

Table 4.7 *The Herald*, 20 September 2018.

8. Zoe Ball wasn't a success story as a Radio 1 DJ. Since that point she has worked at XFM and deputised for Ken Bruce, which means she inherits his massive audience. And her fame/success was to a very large extent predicated on her Loaded magazine image.
9. Ball arrived on national radio amidst a clatter of beer cans and a haze of smoke. The original ladette was defined by her 1999 wedding photograph in which she wears a stetson, a crop top shirt, jeans, and carries a bottle of Jack Daniels while puffing on a Marlboro.
10. She admits to cultivating this image. 'I thought that if I shocked enough people, they would sit up and take notice,' she said at the time. 'I think I was trying to create a new persona.'
11. What was wrong with old one, Zoe? Not strong enough on its own to get you the job?
12. Yes, the presenter is 47 now and the hell-raising days are most likely gone. But take that laddishness away and with it goes headlines, which Radio 2 loves and the prankish, impish Evans has provided.
13. What is there about Zoe Ball that can offer breakfast listeners some snap and crackle with their pop? Is she a poster girl for feminism? Is she anything more than a mother of two who lives in a picturesque village in East Sussex just up the road from Dame Vera Lynn and declares she loves her vegetable garden and plants? Should she not be Beechgrove Garden bound instead, where she can wear a flat cap and get up to her oxters in coo dung?

In context, we can see that the term 'ladette' is actually being used in a negative way by Beacom. In paragraph 8, he describes her appearance as being inappropriate for a traditional wedding, and in paragraph 12 reframes this as 'hell-raising'. When the behaviour is applied to Evans, it is more positively labelled 'prankish, impish'. The disapproval of ladette behaviour is based on the lack of parity in perceptions of such behaviour when exhibited by either gender. In fact, Beacom then goes on to domesticate Ball by referring to her status as a mother and gardener (paragraph 13), something that is emphasized in the final sentence of that paragraph by the reference to a popular Scottish TV gardening show, Beachgrove Garden, and further linked to the reader by the use of the Scots dialect 'coo' for cow.

In terms of verb structural choices, we can see the use of both active and passive voices. In English, the standard sentence structure features subject – verb – object, or SVO. The subject or active agent carries out the action on an object or affected agent. This is referred to as active voice, and these are a few examples.

Subject	verb	object
She	inherits	his massive audience
She	admits to cultivating	this image

Passive voice re-orders this construction with the subject or active agent following the verb, or being omitted entirely. For example:

Object	verb	± subject
His massive audience	is inherited	by Ball
This image	is admitted to have been cultivated	by Ball

Passive voice can be used strategically to highlight an action rather than the actor, for example, in this story the opening paragraph: 'It's been claimed she was one of five female favourites for the job.' There is no indication of where this claim comes from. The source is hidden as it is unattributed, so the focus becomes that of the claim, on which this story is based. However, if we look more closely at the verbs used in the story, we can see that there is a deeper reading available, such that it becomes clear that it is not just the case that active and passive voices can reveal something about how gender is represented.

Drawing on MAK Halliday's function grammar, we can divide verbs into the broad categories of actional and relational, before subdividing them further (Table 4.8).

Table 4.8

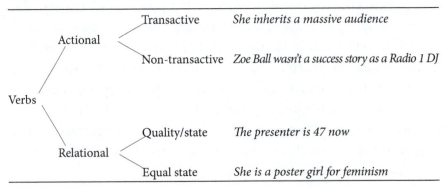

As the names suggest, actional verbs carry with them some sort of physical action. Verbs which grammatically carry out an action on another agent/object are called 'transactive' verbs. In the example above, Ball is carrying out an action that is affecting the audience. However, grammatically, these actional verbs do not all necessarily carry an action on another object/agent. Such verbs are referred to as being 'non-transactive' and an example of such a verb is given above in the sentence 'Zoe Ball wasn't a success story as a Radio 1 DJ'. Here, the action attached to Ball is offered as having no effect on anyone or anything else. There is a simple test to find out whether an actional verb is transactive or non-transactive: if the sentence can be made passive, then it is a transactive verb. In the example above, the passive voice construction of the transactive verb would be 'The massive audience was inherited'. This may sound clumsy, but still makes grammatical sense. On the other hand, the non-transactive utterance 'Zoe Ball wasn't a success story as a Radio 1 DJ' cannot be made sense of in passive voice ('*a success story as a Radio 1 DJ was not').

The so-called relational verbs are verbs which do not carry an action with them, but instead offer information about the quality or state of the active agent, or else offer details of equal state. These verb constructions cannot be made passive.

From this, we can begin to see that non-transactive verbs, and both sorts of relational verbs carry minimal effect with them: they are only affecting the person who is carrying out the action. We can see how this relates to representations of women in the media if we return to *The Herald* story about Zoe Ball. As noted above, much of the story is written in active voice with strategic use of passive voice. However, if we look at the verbs in more detail, then we can see how something more complicated is going on.

Sarah Brown with Zoe Ball, in the eight paragraph, is represented using transactive verbs in active voice. As noted earlier, these verbs work to place her in a role that lacks success in the role for which she is being proposed. If we look at paragraph 11, and then compare this with paragraph 5, we can see that it is not Ball, but her radio show that is 'holding its own', with the double negative 'Ball isn't a bad presenter', showing only grudging acknowledgement of her talent to frame this.

Elsewhere, Ball is linked with the transactive verb construction of 'admitting' and 'said', and this is followed by the only direct quotation from her in paragraph 13. The quotation itself, if we look at it, appears to reinforce the point that Beacom is making about Ball's lack of suitability for the job, but in context, we can see that the quotation is actually nearly twenty years old. However, it is used by Beacom in another synthesized dialogue with, but here with Ball herself.

One final strategy that is widespread in print media, and indeed across media, is that of double-voicing. This is often used to state an argument or point that is at odds with dominant discourses, and in this case, related to the dominant discourse of gender equality. Judith Baxter (2014) describes this as a complex strategy that can be used to avoid overt confrontation (such as overt sexism). She comments that 'double-voicing is closely implicated with the ways in which power relations are constructed between speakers according to the interplay of social categories such as gender, age, ethnicity, profession and status' (2014: 3). Such strategies include token agreement, which is what we see Beacom doing here in paragraph 15:

> Yes, the presenter is 47 now and the hell-raising days are most likely gone. But take that laddishness away and with it goes headlines, which Radio 2 loves and the prankish, impish Evans has provided.

The 'yes, but' frame is part of what Baxter describes as the concession/constraint nature of double-voicing which allows you a speaker to acknowledge the agenda of an interlocutor whilst also retaining their own agenda. Here, Beacom is acknowledging the argument that his evidence of Ball's lack of suitability is based on her 1999 marriage photo, but then returning to his claim that there is nothing beyond that persona if you do take that away. He has adopted this to make the same point in paragraph 5 ('Ball isn't a bad presenter [...] but it's an excuse in shallow cheeriness'), and particularly in paragraph 7 where he addresses the issue of gender equality in broadcast media ('yes, push women in broadcasting to succeed. But to not consider a male appointment is risible').

Overall, if we look at how these women are framed, we find that they are supportive in both the grammatical sense and the pragmatic sense. The attention to the visual appearance of the female politicians, as seen here in the reference to Esther McVey outfit, can be related to the grace and elegance expected of women in the stereotypes outlined above. This representation of Ball here has an emphasis on domesticity (or perceived lack of it) as we found when discussing Marina Wheeler and Zoe Ball, and passivity aligned with visual appearance can also be seen in the story about Kylie Minogue that we looked at earlier.

Sexuality

A final point about the way in which print media language can be used to reflect developments in society's attitudes relating to gender and sexuality can be seen in the growing awareness of non-binary and trans rights. Famously, Caitlyn Jenner charted her transition through a reality TV series, *I Am Cait* (2015–16) and in so doing has brought a greater awareness and acceptance of non-binary and trans issues. In terms of print media, this has been manifest in debates relating to the use of pronouns to refer to a report's subjects. English, like other Germanic languages, distinguishes sex using third person singular pronouns (Talbot 2020), however there is no third person singular gender-neutral pronoun in common usage. The third person plural 'they' is increasingly used by non-binary, genderqueer and genderfluid people (amongst others) to refer to themselves, nevertheless this is far from ideal when there is a lack of a singular gender neutral pronoun. Theoretically, the use of the impersonal pronoun 'it' could be used, however this is extremely problematic as it might be gender neutral but it carries with it fundamental connotations of dehumanization and has often been used as a derogatory term for trans people. There have been attempts to introduce third person pronouns, for which Crystal (2007) provides a list of examples. However, in their study, Senden et al. (2015) found the introduction of a gender neutral pronoun into a language is often met with hostility and can take years to become more generally accepted, something that is typical of a generally conservative approach to language and language change. However, the argument that it is 'ungrammatical' is largely redundant as in the English language it is common for us to refer to someone as 'they' if we are unaware of their gender or wish to be inclusive. For example, in university documentation, we may find the warning 'Any student who hands their work in late risks failing'. This is perfectly understandable, and is also inclusive.

It could be argued that pronoun usage imposes a gendered identity onto people as it becomes extremely difficult to speak about a third person without assigning them male or female, particularly over a long period of time. In addition, the linguistic assignment of sex carries with it the presumptions of societal gender norms and expectations, which supports Butler's (1990) argument that the idea of gender is ingrained into humans by the repetition and normalization of gendered acts. This is at the heart of a trans person's decision about which pronoun they choose. It is increasingly common for people to declare their preferred pronouns in their automated email signatures and in their Twitter handles, where she/her, he/his, they/their draw on existing pronouns. As mentioned above, there are attempts to introduce new pronouns, such as zhe/zhir, which combine the phonetic properties of existing pronouns with innovative spelling and so moved away from the binary gendered norms that Butler highlights as being socially driven.

As such, it could be said that it is quite straightforward to use appropriate pronouns for people who are trans or non-binary. Indeed, in September 2019, singer Sam Smith announced on social media that they would prefer to be referred to by gender neutral pronouns they/them. Trans activists such as Caitlyn Jenner have argued that the use of pronouns is so important that anyone who does state a preference for specific pronouns should have this decision honoured, even when referring to them historically (see Ward, 2020 for a more detailed discussion of this). If we think of this in terms of speech acts and Searle's point about felicity conditions, the right to declare your gendered pronoun preference is one that the individual is warranted to make and it should be respected in news copy. However, reporting of Smith's announcement occasionally misgenders them. For example, in the online newspaper, *The Spectator*, on 17 September reporter Andrew Doyle wrote:

> Singer Sam Smith has announced that from now on his pronouns are 'they/them', sparking an overdue conversation about the social justice movement's ongoing efforts to influence the way we speak. Of course Smith is free to make his request – just as we are free to decide whether or not to accede – but with such attempts to skip over the natural process of language evolution, where does that leave the teachers whose job it is to uphold basic grammatical standards?

As an item of opinion journalism, this extract enacts the linguistic debate it discusses. The extract's rejection of Smith's request, using 'he/him' throughout the article, is initially framed as a welcome opportunity ('an overdue conversation') to consider the efforts of non-binary people to be recognized in language. However, in an example of double voicing, Doyle concedes through an axiomatic marker ('of course') that Smith is 'free to make [their] request', but then rejects this with the counter argument that 'we' are free to ignore it. This is reinforced with reference to the 'natural process' of language change, which runs counter to Butler's argument. This opening paragraph finishes with an interpolatory question that assumes the reader will agree that the use of they/them flouts grammatical proprietary. This reflects the findings of Senden et al. (2015) in their exploration of the resistance of linguistic change.

A more considered report on Smith's announcement came in *The Guardian*, where Laura Snapes's report fluently used the they/them pronouns (13 September 2019).

> In their Instagram post, Smith said they were 'at no stage just yet to eloquently speak at length about what it means to be non-binary' but that their intention was to be 'visible and open'.
>
> Smith pledged to answer questions that fans may have, and cited 'activists and leaders of the non-binary/trans community' that had aided their understanding of gender identity, among them the actor Laverne Cox, model Munroe Bergdorf and the charities Stonewall, Glaad and Mermaids.

The fact *The Spectator* and other newspapers, such as the right-leaning *The Sun*, chose to ignore Smith's wishes whilst the left-leaning *Guardian*, amongst others, acceded to them reveals how issues of language and sexuality in print media are in a state of development. This reflects the developing acceptance of non-binary sexuality in society, but also stresses the opportunity journalism has to hasten this development.

Conclusion

In looking at the language of newspaper journalism, we have examined the structures and lexical choices of headlines and news stories. We have suggested that one of the key considerations in looking at newspaper discourse in a market such as Britain is the difference between popular and quality newspapers. But we have also argued that discourses of gender and identity are important in understanding newspapers, often bound up with parallel discourses of celebrity and popular culture. These representations, we have found, are apparent both in lexical choices over naming and describing participants in a story and in the grammatical structures within which their activities are described.

Sports journalism

Introduction

In this chapter we are going to look at the particular practices of language associated with sports journalism. Sports coverage and reporting are types of journalistic endeavour that occupies a difficult and sometimes contentious place in the news industry. In an article arguing for the importance of sports journalism, David Rowe (2007: 386) reflects regretfully on its characterization as the 'toy department' of the newsroom: where a male-dominated culture is free to indulge in pastimes, confecting controversy from frivolity. In fact, and contrary to these prejudices, Rowe argues that in terms of its capacity to deal with social and political issues and the degree of professionalism required, sports journalism outperforms many of the more outwardly 'serious' genres. And as we will go on to see, many other scholars argue that the study of sports journalism reveals the involvement of news media in discourses of militarism, race and nation (see Blain and O'Donnell, 1998; Garland and Rowe, 1999; Maguire, Poulton and Possamai, 1999).

In terms, also, of the diversity of forms it introduces to the study of news, we will see there is much to be gained from the study of sports journalism. For example, we will look at the peculiar forms of linguistic performance in live commentary, separating out the component types of speech in live commentary and showing how these types foster hierarchies in both the expression and organization of the account of the sporting event. This leads us into the brave new world of online sports commentary, where the impact of technology is at its most apparent. We will also look at the capacity of sports journalism to promote formations of national identity. Looking at the coverage of international football, we will show how popular historical discourses unite to motivate a sense of national togetherness, against an excluded and marginalized 'other'. As we will see throughout this chapter, sports journalism expresses far more than our relationship with sport, and produces a vivid expression of our relationship with identity.

Sports commentary

To begin with, we are going to look at 'live' commentary of sports events. Live commentary has a number of exceptional qualities. Firstly, more than any other form of journalistic comments and description, it deals with what Stephanie Marriott (2007: 76) describes as the '*now*-moment in which stuff is happening'. It therefore demands a reflexivity and responsiveness unusual even for an industry fixated with timeliness. Secondly, live commentary uses this lexicon of responsiveness to generate excitement in the audience; often by 'communicating a sense of high-drama in the events of screen [or on radio or webcast]' (Rowe, 2004: 118). Garry Whannel (1992: 26) describes this as 'on the one hand the impulse to describe the scene, give the audience an accurate picture, and on the other the impulse to get people involved, keep up the interest, add suspense, shape the material and highlight the action'. It is this pressure to avoid a deadening silence, according to Rowe (2004: 119), that gives rise to so many of the apparent 'inanities and infelicities' that are routinely used to characterize sports commentary and subject it to occasional ridicule.

However, we will see that commentary is far more organized and open to analysis than its everyday criticism within the industry and amongst sports aficionados would have us believe. Typically, commentary has a structure and contains linguistic features that can be applied across the treatment of different sports. As Daniel Dayan and Elihu Katz (1992: 30) point out, sports contests are mediated 'events' that have to be made meaningful and placed in context through their commitment to form and the manner of their 'telling'. We have mentioned other books that have looked at the use of 'liveness' in sports commentary (Marriott, 2007) and the use of direct address (Whannel, 1992). We will follow

Judy Delin's linguistic exploration of sports commentary, eventually linking this to how community is created, as we looked at in Chapters 3 and 4.

Beginning by looking at the structure of the commentary, we can see that there are four main types of utterances:

1. Narration: time-critical description of what is happening play-by-play;
2. Evaluating: giving opinions about play, players, teams, referee decisions, etc.;
3. Elaborating: providing background information about team and player records, the ground, the crowd; speculating on motives and thoughts of players;
4. Summarizing: giving occasional overviews of play and results so far (Delin, 2000: 46).

If we are to assume that the main purpose of a live commentary is to describe what is happening, then narration is the form of utterance best placed to accomplish this. The live-ness of a sporting event is encompassed in narration through a description of what is going on at the time of play. However, the three other main types of utterances tend to be deployed during quieter periods of an ongoing event, or when there has been a particularly noteworthy occurrence on the pitch that requires more than a basic, time-critical description. These types of utterances tend to be more explicitly subjective, often drawing the reputation and expertise of the commentator, as suggested by their labels as evaluative, elaborative or summative. Chovanec (2009) has commented on the fluency of the speakers as they shift between these roles, exploring where there are shifts between what he terms primary layer of narration (the game-related talk) and the secondary layer (utterances unrelated to events in the game).

Commentary: managing styles

By looking in some detail at the different utterance types in a football commentary, we can see how there are actually two different roles ascribed to the two commentators, but that switching between styles is far more complex and responsive than these roles suggest, as Chovanec has observed. The transcript here is from the Germany–England match at Bloemfontein in the 2010 World Cup finals, and to start with we are going to look in some detail at a stretch of commentary taken from early in the game before either team had scored, also bringing in examples from a part of the match where the commentators are discussing a disallowed goal. The match was broadcast live on BBC1 on Sunday, 27 June 2010, and we are going to be looking at the commentary team of Guy Mowbray, who is a long-standing professional sports journalist working for the BBC, and retired professional footballer, Mark Lawrenson. This arrangement has become customary for live sporting events in British broadcasting: to have two members of the 'commentary team', one of whom is often a former or current professional in the relevant sport.

In an embodiment of Delin's (2000: 46) categorization, only one of the commentators is called upon to narrate, whilst the second commentator is only called upon to evaluate during slower parts of the game, and provide occasional elaborative and summative utterances. In addition to Chovanec's primary and secondary layers of narration, Kuipar and Lewis draw this distinction as between 'play-by-play commentary' and 'colour'. In this case, the professional journalist, here Guy Mowbray, exclusively provides the narration, whilst the retired footballer, Mark Lawrenson, provides additional information which can draw on his experiences as a player at the highest level. Important too for the relationship between the commentators and the event is the extent of the audience's access. We are going to look here at the traditional broadcasting of sport, but later in this chapter we will look at the greater integration of audiences through innovations in digital journalism. Kuipar and Lewis (2013) point to the pronounced difference between television (with images and sound) and radio (with just sound), but even in our televisual example the visual images made available to the viewer are not under the control of the BBC, but are shot by FIFA-nominated camera operators and directors.

In the extract that follows (Table 5.1), we can see all four utterance types, as set out above (pauses are indicated by bracketed stops and then by numbers of seconds):

Table 5.1 Commentary on 2010 World Cup Finals, BBC1, Sunday, 2 June 2010. Extract 1.

Mowbray	Rooney (4) ups it to Terry (.) I'm not sure he quite wanted that (2)	1
	Ashley Cole (3) Vincent Ozil (.) German born (.) Turkish father (.)	2
	is a very clever footballer (.) only twenty one	3
		4
Lawrenson	There's a few Polish born as well isn't there in this team	5
		6
Mowbray	Yeh it really is the the rainbow nation this Germany squad (4) like	7
	for us with South Africans on the cricket field I suppose (4) here's	8
	Defoe (.) now Glen Johnson (4) Milner (4) in towards Defoe (.) it	9
	was a good header from Mertesacker (.) Defoe was trying to let it	10
	run for Rooney	11
		12
Lawrenson	The good thing as well is that Boateng really just let Milner cross	13
	it	14

We can immediately see the need to switch between types. Mowbray's first utterance on line 1 ('Rooney (4) ups it to Terry') is an example of narration, describing the live action. However, his next utterance on that line is evaluative as he speculates on whether the recipient of the pass welcomed the move ('I'm not sure he quite wanted that'). Mowbray then reverts to narrative in line two ('Ashely Cole (3) Vincent Ozil') before switching to elaboration, where he gives us more information about the German player ('German born (.) Turkish father'), before immediately switching again to evaluation to offer his opinion that Ozil is a 'very clever footballer'. Lawrenson's interjection on line 5 is elaborative ('there's a few Polish born as well'), although it is framed as a question through the tag 'isn't it', thereby inviting Mowbray to respond with a further elaborative utterance on line 7. There is then a four-second gap in the commentary on line 8 before Mowbray continues with the narrative utterance describing the game on lines 9–10, before then offering evaluation on lines 10–11. Lawrenson then comes in on line 13 with a summary of what has happened in the last few minutes on the pitch.

There are also indicators of the relative spontaneity of that is necessary to live commentary. At point, we can see Mowbray having to repair what may be unkindly interpreted as a discriminatory utterance that has been collaborated on by the two commentators on lines 2–7, where the ethnic origins of several of the German squad have been discussed, and where Mowbray begins to ameliorate possible misreadings by referring to the German team as a 'rainbow nation' (line 7). After his initial intervention and four-second pause, Mowbray then draws on a collective knowledge of the ethnicity of the English cricket team, linking the commentary with wider debates about the inclusion of players who are not born in England in the team. Hinting at a pattern we will return to later in the chapter, there is a clear distinction between 'us' (the English, to whom the analogy applies) and the interloping 'them' (those South Africans included in the England team).

What remains as the most rigid component of the relationship between style and commentator is that narration is the exclusive preserve of the professional journalist in the commentary team. Moreover, Delin suggests, other than the occasion lapse or breakdown of roles, the exclusivity of the 'main' commentator in describing the action is common to live commentary across sports.

Commentary: managing speakers

In circumstances where there are two people commentating on a game, we need to look at how speaker change is managed. Often this is simply by switching from one type of utterance to another, marked by a gap of a few seconds, as we have seen in the above extract. However, if we go back to turn-taking, as we looked at in Chapter 2, we can see how the normal rules of successful speaker management apply (see Graddol et al., 1994: 162). While there are discrete activities, usually two or more of these turn-taking cues occur at the same time:

- Explicit nomination: speaker A can name speaker B explicitly, so giving them an explicit cue;
- Pause: a gap allowing other speaker to come in and speak;
- Syntactic completion: there is a clear end to the utterance indicated by grammatical structure;
- Intonation: falling intonation, or rising for a question, may indicate turn completion.

In addition, the direction of gaze or the exchange of looks may also play a role, although even in television commentary where the cameras focus on the sporting action, the analyst is in no position to gauge the role of the gaze between the interactants (even though studio-based panel discussions can offer such an opportunity).

What is remarkable about much sports commentary is that there is very little overlap between speakers. Where overlap does occur, it tends to be at periods of heightened excitement and tends to be very brief. Here is a short extract (Table 5.2) of overlap which occurs in the part of the commentary following England's disallowed goal, and so is a period of confusion:

Table 5.2 Commentary on 2010 World Cup Finals, BBC1, Sunday, 2 June 2010. Extract 2.

Lawrenson	What is it FIFA don't want (1) technology (.) thanks very much	1
	Sepp Blatter (4)	2
		3
Mowbray	England could /lose this	4
		5
Lawrenson	/Well I hope he's here and he's squirming in his	6
	seat by the way	7

The overlap on line 4 by Lawrenson shows him attempting to add to his indignant evaluation of a perceived lack of assiduousness on the part of the governing body of world football, FIFA, in particular the president, Sepp Blatter. Lawrenson's passionate disgust at the inaction of this individual overrides the conventions of sports commentary and, when Mowbray attempts to change the evaluation to a closer focus on the England team on line 4 after a four-second pause, and Lawrenson continues his diatribe on Blatter through lines 6 and 7. Mowbray concedes the floor to Lawrenson by not elaborating on his speculative evaluation ('England could lose this'), perhaps explained in this particular case by Mowbray's role as journalist discouraging from giving voice to his personal frustration. Mowbray therefore steps back and allows former-footballer Lawrenson to continue to express his annoyance as an elaborating utterance.

It is important to note that these cues are *opportunities* for the other commentator to take the floor rather than commands or obligations for them to do so. Most of the time, speaker change occurs without a discernible gap where there is a collaborative evaluative or elaborative utterance. But elsewhere, there are utterances which follow longer gaps of several seconds, which are not always taken as potential opportunities for change of turn. Indeed, within this television commentary, we can see many examples of lengthy pauses where there is no speaker change. For example, in the following section (Table 5.3) we can see Mowbray commenting on an unsuccessful appeal against an off-side decision (line 1), before resuming narration (lines 1–5) then further evaluation (lines 5–10).

Table 5.3 Commentary on 2010 World Cup Finals, BBC1, Sunday, 2 June 2010. Extract 3.

Mowbray	His claim was the biggest thing (.) passed back [shots of	1
	German corner] Schweinsteiger (.) out comes James (.) that's a	2
	good solid catch (5) gone for the punt (.) Friedrich's touch (.)	3
	picked out by Baoteng (.) there's Schweinsteiger (.) finds	4
	Muller (2) just swapping sides for a moment (3) Schweinsteiger	5
	plays it against Johnson to get Germany the throw-in (6) young	6
	or not (.) there's arguably just as much pressure on this German	7
	team as the er more experienced England players (.) they've	8
	only once failed to reach the last eight of a World Cup and that	9
	was in nineteen thirty eight	10
		11
Lawrenson	I think it's the same for both isn't it (.) we expect England to	12
	win and the Germans expect their team to win (4)	13
		14
Mowbray	Can't both be happy at the end of the day (2)	15
		16
Lawrenson	[laughing] Right (4)	17
		18
Mowbray	This is going through and Friedrich and Neuer will be happy	19
	for it to do so (4)	20

Whether or not a cue to take the floor is accepted depends largely on the development of the dialogue between the commentators, and whether disagreements have arisen. Mowbray's syntactic completion of his elaborative utterance on line 10 is not followed by a noticeable gap, but Lawrenson picks up on this elaborative utterance and offers his own elaboration to balance out the implied assertion that there is more pressure on the German players to win, owing to their long record of World Cup success. In keeping with the politeness strategies outlined by Brown and Levinson (1987), his is turned into a question through the use of the tag 'isn't it' (line 12), followed by a short gap, which is not taken up by Mowbray, so occasioning further elaboration by Lawrenson. This embellishment is continued after a gap of four seconds, when it takes the floor to imply that Mowbray there has to be one winner (something viewers would be aware of, giving the match taking place in the knock-out stages of the tournament), by noting that one team/nation will be disappointed. Another gap of two seconds is needed before Lawrenson concurs, which is then there is silence of four seconds before Mowbray resumes the narration of events on the pitch. Here, then, we can see the commentators cooperatively filling the gap in the narration during a 'quiet' period of play, although it is apparent that cues are not always taken-up, and other strategies can be employed to keep the commentary going.

Hierarchies of utterance and commentator

A chief task of commentary is to appraise the audience of what is going on. On this basis, narration takes priority over other types of utterance. Occasionally, this ranking is manifest in the professional journalist commentator having warrant to resume narration if something remarkable happens on the pitch whilst the pundit commentator is evaluating, elaborating or summarizing. More frequently, though, this precedence of narration is clear from the disfluencies in the talk, where a contribution by the pundit is not enjoined by the journalist commentator, who instead resumes narration of events on the pitch. Here is a brief example of this (Table 5.4):

Table 5.4 Commentary on 2010 World Cup Finals, BBC1, Sunday, 2 June 2010. Extract 4.

Lawrenson	It was one of the things about Slovenia the other night was that	1
	England played the diagonal ball very well (2)	2
		3
Mowbray	It's Boateng's throw (3) Terry (6) Rooney didn't know where the	4
	ball was (3) then Johnson (3) Germany's goal kick (8)	5

Contrary to norms of politeness, we can see that Lawrenson's summary of a previous match is not continued by Mowbray, who instead resumes the narration of the on-pitch action, choosing not to develop the topic of England's previous strategies further at this point.

However, as we can also see from this interruption, such hierarchies of prominence apply to the commentators as well as the utterance. While the use of names to manage turn-taking is quite rare, here (Table 5.5) we find an example when Mowbray calls on Lawrenson to offer his opinion as former player of the likely state-of-mind of the England players following a disallowed goal:

Table 5.5 Commentary on 2010 World Cup Finals, BBC1, Sunday, 2 June 2010. Extract 5.

Mowbray	It's pay-back for the Germans (5) well they've got to use that Mark haven't they?	1 2 3
Lawrenson	Yes (.) most definitely (6)	4

Delin's analysis of football commentary points to unequal power relations between the two commentators, in an arrangement where the professional journalist/commentator occupies a position of dominance. One sign of this supremacy that Delin highlights is the use of nomination by the professional journalist towards the co-commentator, where they call upon them by name to speak. More common than this, however, are a cooperative and complex set of arrangements, involving, although as we have seen, the unequal distribution of types of utterance, in a way that favours the commentator.

There are, however, occasional elements of narration from the former player that we can point to. The following section of commentary (Table 5.6) came soon after England's disallowed goal and follows a heated discussion on the use of goal-line technology:

Table 5.6 Commentary on 2010 World Cup Finals, BBC1, Sunday, 2 June 2010. Extract 6.

Mowbray	Well I don't care what vantage point you've got inside this stadium (1) but you could see that (4) it's out (.) and it's a Germany throw (5)	Ball crossed out for German throw.	1 2 3 4 5

Lawrenson	Well the crowd are giving the referee abuse but (1) if you don't see it (.) you can't give it (5) she's telling him (3)	Shots of throw-in with England supporters clearly shouting at referee behind player	6 7 8 9

Here, we can see Mowbray continuing an elaboration on the referee failing to see the ball cross the line for a goal, before returning to narration on line 3 to resume his live commentary of events on the pitch. However, the former player Lawrenson sees activities off the pitch that deserve remark, where an England fan is seen gesticulating behind the German player about to take the throw-in. Although play is not actually taking place at this time, Lawrenson's comment on lines 8–9 – 'she's telling him' – could be regarded as being a narrative utterance. However, as soon as play resumes, Mowbray immediately positions himself at the centre of the narrative frame.

This also calls our attention to the role of visual images on screen. On the one hand, commentary often performs a deictic function; 'pointing' to something or someone within the visual field (of the fan, 'she's telling him'). Also, the visual images mean that the lengthy gaps in the commentary do not figure as 'dead air', as the silences allow that the viewers can see for themselves that there may be a lull in the action on the pitch, without having this having rendered as an explicit part of the narration (such as retrieving the ball or organizing players for 'set pieces', such as corners, throw-ins and free kicks). In the case of radio sports commentary, the 'dead ball' time is usually filled with evaluative, elaborative or summarizing utterances, or, famously in cricket commentary, with talk on other matters altogether.

Overall, the commentary arrangement is therefore a collaborative one, with recognized power relations in place, mainly through the convention of priority being given to narrative utterances, and these being uttered only by the professional journalist commentator. This is an example of what Sacks and colleagues (1974) suggest as the ability of speakers to identify turn types (here, based on the four main types of utterances) and so understand how turn-taking can be managed where there is the possibility of interruption and overlap.

Commentary and shared emotions

We have spoken about cooperation between the commentators. The commentators also act in accord by sharing humorous exchanges, engaging in **banter**. An example of this is to be found in Transcript 3, lines 12–17, beginning with Lawrenson's question to Mowbray 'I think it's the same for both isn't it' and then Lawrenson laughing at Mowbray's reply. This display of shared humour in their commentary suggests to the overhearing audience that they are in the company of people who are not only knowledgeable about the sport, but are of a friendly and light-hearted disposition (where humour is also used as a form of positive politeness).

These performances of shared emotion also extend the relationship of the commentators to the teams and to the community they shared with viewers. The dialogue between the two commentators allows the overhearing audience access to an informed discussion involving regular participants who are assuming shared knowledge of the teams and previous matches. This sense of community is also clear through an expression of shared incredulity following England's disallowed goal (Table 5.7):

Table 5.7 Commentary on 2010 World Cup Finals, BBC1, Sunday 2 June, 2010. Extract 7.

Lawrenson	Everyone is in a state of shock aren't they	1
		2
Mowbray	Well it's quite incredible (.) we had all the talk in the build-up to the	3
	World Cup (.) FIFA issued their edict a couple of months ago (1) end	4
	of debate (2) no goal-line technology (3)	5
		6
Lawrenson	What's the profit they'll make from this World Cup? (2)	7
		8
Mowbray	A frightening amount (4) the linesman from Uruguay not Russia (5)	9

Here, the turn-taking is clearly identified by the questions posed by Lawrenson (lines 1 and 7), and amounts to an exchange of expressions of disbelief. These are underpinned by a shared sense of injustice that is directed at the governing body of world football and its decision not to use the sort of technology that the commentators are certain would have allowed the England goal to stand ('FIFA issued their edict a couple of months ago (1) end of debate (2) no goal-line technology'). Thus the criticisms are directed not at the referee (Lawrenson spends quite some time defending the referee who had not been placed to actually see the ball cross the line), but rather the alleged incompetence and money-grabbing in FIFA.

The community here is forged through knowledge as well as shared indignation: in particular, the reference on line 9 to the linesman being 'from Uruguay not Russia'. To out-group members, this might appear to be a confusing reference that has little apparent relevance to the game or the discussion at this point. However, in-group England football fans would be familiar with the historical reference of the 'Russian Linesman' as alluding to linesman Tofik Bakhramov, who confirmed to the referee in the 1966 World Cup Final that the controversial Geoff Hurst goal in extra time had crossed the line. This shared knowledge on the circumstances of the 1966 emerges again in Mowbray's comment in Transcript 4 that the incident under discussion is 'pay-back for the Germans'. We will see later in this chapter, newspaper headlines give rise to such references, particularly in the case of sporting events, as they are central to the sense of community that sports journalism is complicit in creating.

Micro linguistic features

From the above, it will now be clear that the micro linguistic features of commentary also contribute to the differences between types of utterance, and we can add a little to this here. We have seen that one of the main functions of narration is to describe who is in control of play. If we look again at the transcripts that feature narration, we can see there are some specific linguistic features that enable us to recognize this. For one, narration is constrained by time, and lengthy pauses indicate either a lull in play or that a particular player has control of the ball. For example, in Transcript 3, we can tell from the lengthy pauses in Mowbray's narration that the ball is in play but possession has not changed, with the longest pause of five seconds indicating that the ball is in the air after the England keeper, David James, has kicked it back down the pitch (referred to here by the colloquial footballing register as 'gone for the punt') (Transcript 3, line 3).

Another feature of the narration is its employment of short noun phrases, primarily the players' names, together with the minimal use of verbs. This is a characteristic quality of sports commentary and calls upon the radio listeners in particular to have a reasonable grasp of the names of the relevant players to at least understand which team has possession. In Transcript 3, for example, the kick by James ends up with Friedrich, and so the viewers have to establish for themselves that possession has changed from England to Germany.

The verb tense in the narration also plays an important role. As this is 'time-critical commentary' (Delin, 2000: 46), it is largely given in present tense. In Delin's discussion of sports commentary (2000: 47), she suggested that the verbs used in narration are not finite (i.e. they do not carry tense), but we can see from the examples here that this is not so exclusively the case. There is an example of a non-finite verb on line 5, where two of the German players are described as 'swapping sides', but other verb choices are finite (Transcript 3 line 4:'finds Muller'; line 6: 'plays it against Johnson'). We can also see that there is a limited use of past tense in the narration, where Mowbray comments on an immediately previous action that has appeared on screen (e.g. Transcript 3 line 1, 'passed back'; line 3 'gone of the punt'). However, the overall impression remains of sense of liveness.

Online reporting of sport: a quest to be part of the action

The live reporting of sport is one of the most interesting aspects of the impact of social media in journalism. The liveness of sport is one of its main appeals, and has been a feature of radio and television broadcasting from their earliest times, not to mention the special place sport has traditionally occupied in the back pages of every newspaper. The possibilities of online journalism have allowed traditional media to embrace liveness in a way that has previously only been possible in broadcast journalism. Sport occupies a unique place in our lives, bringing people together in a social space, and in a virtual social space. As Andrew Crisell points out:

> Live sports coverage is nothing less than news in the making, for, unlike conventional news broadcasts, which for the most part give a live account of events that have recently happened, its events are unfolding before our eyes and will have an unknown outcome.

(2012: 45)

This liveness in broadcasting has more recently been put to the test in terms of its accessibility by the desire of sports bodies to increase their revenue by selling the broadcast rights to pay-to-view TV channels. The viewing of sport is thus restricted to those who can afford to pay for the privilege, either in physically attending the event or by subscribing to the relevant provider. One way the wider media has found to by-pass this visual restriction comes in their use of online media, where liveness can be maintained through interactive 'live' web sites as well as Twitter accounts devoted to the sport (see Kroon, 2014, 2017). James Blake (2017: 132) argues that social media technology has been used most enthusiastically in sport, as it provides a means for sports fans to express their identity and community in ways that are otherwise denied them through ticketing policies and viewing rights. Even where fans are watching or listening to their teams play through traditional means such as TV or radio, they are still using their mobile devices to interact with others in a way that enhances rather than distracts from their experiences. Gerard Goggin (2013) has referred to the special place sport has in social media owing the 'symbiotic' relationship between sport and mobile phones. According to Goggin, 'Apps play a heightened role in the prosaic logistics and coordination of individuals and groups participating in and watching sport' (2013: 30). Apps that are linked to official accounts such as BBC Sport or other news outlets can be linked to 'notifications' on mobile devices, tailored to such a level as individual users can select which teams' activities they want to receive updates about to their home screen. This all enhances the sense of nowness, with fans being made to feel that they are part of a wider community of people who share their interest (Kroon, 2017).

In order to explore this further, we will look at the online coverage of the first morning's play of the cricket tournament known as the 'The Ashes', which is a series of matches played by England and Australia every two years, regarded as being the pinnacle of cricketing prizes. Since public service broadcaster, the BBC, lost the TV broadcasting rights for this cricket tournament, it has devoted its resources to supporting the remaining radio broadcast rights (through BBC Radio 5 Live and the associated 'Test Match Special' team [TMS], which has its own Twitter account as befits something that is close to a national institution), and has also developed the coverage of this through the BBC Sport website. Newspapers such as *The Guardian* and *The Times* in the UK also have a similar set-up of online live reporting of this tournament. In each case, the same strategies are used as for coverage of other live sporting events, but in the case of cricket, there is the additional coverage found in BBC radio.

The particular event that is test cricket, a match that can take up to five days to reach a conclusion, means that there are frequent lulls in action where fans can engage with online media without actually missing much of the on-field action. This is a greatly expanded version of the 'dead ball' time we saw in the football commentary earlier.

If we begin with the Twitter account for BBC Sport, we can see that early in the first day of the match they are trying to create a sense of involvement and excitement, even though it is several hours before the match is due to start. There is a consistent use of the present tense to highlight the 'nowness' of the event (something Marriot [2007] points out is found across the spectrum when reporting 'live' events), even before it has actually started. In this first tweet (Figure 5.1), there is a close-up picture of the heads of the two team

BBC Sport ✔ @BBCSport · 1h   ⌄

Who's ready? 🏏 🔥

#TheAshes

bbc.in/2SUfPt4

   ♡ 4   ⟲ 30   ♡ 174   ⬆

Figure 5.1 BBC Sport tweet.

captains, separated by a flaming set of cricket stumps (which is the literal origin of The Ashes tournament). The tweet text takes the form of a question, 'Who's ready?', followed by an emoji of a cricket bat and ball and some flames. There is a hashtag for the 'TheAshes' and a hyperlink to the BBC sport web site. In this way, the tweet is both searchable through its use of the tournament name in its hashtag and interactive through the use of the hashtag to attract users to the broader media presence. The followers of BBC Sport are being encouraged to both interact with the tweet (through 'liking' it) and click on the hyperlink to the web site.

The tweets by BBC Sport routinely feature emoji. This gives them a colourful, quirky appeal that would attract the attention of those scrolling through Twitter. Emoji have developed very rapidly as a form of communication that often runs in parallel with conventional written text, but can also take the place of conventional text. As Seargeant has pointed out (2019: 6), emoji have developed to 'compensate for the way that computer-mediated messaging can sometimes tend towards the emotionally blunt'. Emoji can be used in one of four ways: as an illustrative image, such as a cup of coffee; as a metaphor, such as a waving hand; as emblematic, such as the much-discussed aubergine; or as an illocutionary image, such as the much-used crying-with-laughter face. In the case of the emoji in the tweet above, it is the combination of cricket bat and ball with flames that when combined is a metaphor for The Ashes.

With one-and-a-half hours to go before the start of the match, there is another tweet that again seeks to engage followers (Figure 5.2). This time there is the explicit reference to the sporting event, now with four photos of the players, including one of the Australian captain holding The Ashes trophy to remind followers of who the current holders of the title are. Again, we can see the use of an interrogative – 'Who's going?' – before a directive to 'send us your photos on your travels/from Edgbaston', a hyperlink to the BBC Sport website, and an assortment of relevant hashtags to the tournament. This time, there is a combination of different uses of emoji, from the metaphorical bat and ball and the camera, to the illustrative 'vs'.

BBC Sport ✔ @BBCSport · 32m   ⌄
🏏 First Ashes Test
England 🆚 Australia

Who's going? Send us your photos on
your travels/from Edgbaston 📸

bbc.in/2SUfPt4

#ashes2019
#bbccricket
#TheAshes

💬 2   🔁 8   ♡ 64   ⬆️

Figure 5.2 BBC Sport tweet.

This attempt to get the public involved in the online community of cricket fans is one that we see in other tweets. For example, BBC Sport retweets one of the TMS tweets (Figure 5.3), promoting the online broadcasts of the commentary.

Directly addressing the unknown followers with the second person pronoun, there is also the use of parenthesis. However, unlike the friendly aside we saw this used for in the magazines explored in Chapter 3, this is akin to the 'small print' as the relevant BBC commentary is not universally accessible. However, this is not elaborated here, but there is a hyperlink to the relevant YouTube channel, along with the hashtags we have seen used

↻ BBC Sport Retweeted

Test Match Special ✔ @bbctms · 4m   ⌄

You can listen to @bbctms overseas
(some restrictions)

🌐 youtube.com/watch?v=d2hEfq...

#BBCCricket #Ashes

💬 4   ↻ 2   ♡ 21   ⬆️

Figure 5.3 BBC Sport re-tweet.

in other tweets. In this way, the hashtags have the dual purpose of allowing linked searches for facts and updates, whilst also forming a sense of co-present reality (Kroon 2017: 674).

The actual live reporting of the match is heralded by various linguistic strategies. In the relevant BBC Sport tweet (Figure 5.4), it is the use of capitalization: 'We're LIVE for the first day of the #Ashes!'. The excitement is emphasized with the two-handed wave emoji.

The Guardian's online coverage also marks the liveness of it (Figure 5.5), with the use of exclamation marks: 'England v Australia: Ashes 2019 first Test, day one – live updates!'

In both cases, the use of capitalization and exclamation points creates a sense of drama and excitement, something that is being generated even before the first ball is bowled.

BBC Sport ✔ @BBCSport · 27m

We're LIVE for the first day of the
#Ashes! 🙌

Australia have won the toss and will bat
first against England at Edgbaston.

📻 Listen to @bbctms on @5liveSport
📱 Live text with in-play highlights 👉
bbc.in/2SXMqOJ

#bbccricket #ENGvAUS

💬 6   🔁 8   ♡ 49   ⬆️

Figure 5.4 BBC Sport tweet.

The web site for BBC Sport has a special page devoted to this match
(Figure 5.6).

The multi-modal character of this page – producing multiple information
streams in a variety of forms – calls upon a high level of literacy on the part of
the user, and requires a creative engagement with this page in its context, and
less of a reliance on established norms of orderly reading. For example, when
we start to explore the text commentary, it requires us to adapt our conventional
reading of top to bottom of page, and engage instead with bottom to top, as
the most recent entries appear at the top of the screen, not at the bottom. The
colour scheme of the page reflects the black and yellow of the BBC Sport brand,
but the main image is of the England players in their cricket whites huddled
together (we return to the topic of branding in the Digital Journalism chapter).

Figure 5.5 *Guardian* sports tweet.

Figure 5.6 BBC Sport Cricket web site.

The text above them on this more static part of the page (updated when users 'refresh' the page) offers details of the event with a summary of the match's current status appearing as a news headline in the centre of the page above the main image (A). Below the image is the more interactive element of the page (B). The use of capitalization here is reserved for 'LIVE' and serves to highlight the nowness of the reporting at the very top of the page (by clicking on the 'LIVE' hyperlink, people who are registered for BBC iPlayer can also access more clips). The page also implicitly creates a sense of co-present community with a constantly updated tally of the number of people who are viewing that page at any one time. There are links to other pages below this, such as details of the 'scorecard', the link to listen to TMS and links to the various journalists and columnists who are part of the BBC Cricket team (C). At the left side of the screen in a more detailed summary of the current state of play, which is updated, then tabs for 'Live reporting by Amy Lofthouse' and 'Scorecard' (D). At the far right of this line is a blue box containing an icon signifying 'message', and the invitation to 'Get involved' (E). This is the link for users to send messages directly to the production team, and as we will see later, these text messages come to form part of the online reporting of the match.

As Montgomery (2019: 82) notes, multi-modality is also concerned in the projection of pitch and tempo, and here (Figure 5.7) online reporting uses capitals to emphasize the drama and excitement of wickets falling. The colour scheme is selected to reflect the team, so in the case of this match, the blue is for England as it is present in the team's badge, whilst yellow is used for Australia as that is a dominant colour on their badge.

Whilst the tweet contains an image of a blue box featuring the English cricket badge and 'WICKET' in large letters in the centre, this capitalization is also found in combination with an exclamation point as the first word in the tweet (Figure 5.8). There is a brief description of the statistics relating to this wicket (with exclamation point to emphasize the drama), then added colour in the form of a description of the crowd's reaction, all in present tense. This applies to both Lofthouse as main commentating contributor to the web site and the other participants. Unlike the spoken sports commentary we looked at earlier, there is no clear distinction made here, although Lofthouse is the one to provide score updates; the more detailed, colourful commentary shares the same linguistic devices as the other participants.

Test Match Special ✔ @bbctms · 5m   ∨

WICKET!

Stuart Broad makes the breakthrough, a
full ball trapping David Warner LBW for 2!

"Cheerio" sing the Edgbaston crowd.

Australia 2-1.

☛ bbc.in/2SXMqOJ

#bbccricket #ENGvAUS #Ashes

♡ 40   ↺ 68   ♡ 367

Figure 5.7 BBC Sport Test Match special tweet.

To return to Chovanec's (2009) discussion of the primary layer of narration
(game-related talk) and secondary layer (utterances unrelated to game events)
that we saw in the spoken football commentary, we can see the same thing
happening, but with additional visual elements. For example, the blue theme
we saw in the Twitter feed is also found in the BBC web site, but there is no
exclamation point and the report is initially more formal and factual than the
tweet. However, instead of a description of the action, there is an exclamatory
point of 'Got him!'. It is only two posts later than we get a reflection of the
action from contributor Tufnell, which is again rendered more dramatic
with an initial 'Brilliant!' and a more judgemental account in that this was a
'fantastic bit of bowling', although his pundit's comment is written in past tense
as he recounts the action with a sense of temporal distance. The sense of drama
and excitement is also being emphasized here by the most recent posting from

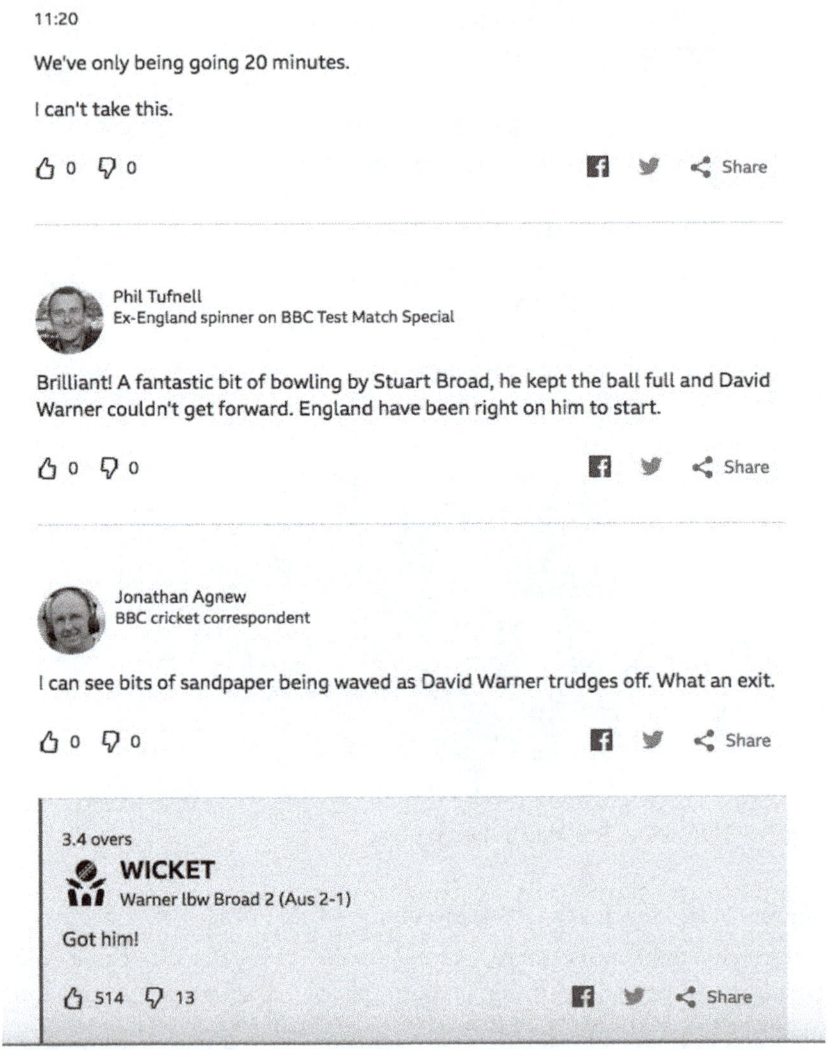

11:20

We've only being going 20 minutes.

I can't take this.

👍 0   👎 0   f 𝕐   ⦉ Share

Phil Tufnell
Ex-England spinner on BBC Test Match Special

Brilliant! A fantastic bit of bowling by Stuart Broad, he kept the ball full and David Warner couldn't get forward. England have been right on him to start.

👍 0   👎 0   f 𝕐   ⦉ Share

Jonathan Agnew
BBC cricket correspondent

I can see bits of sandpaper being waved as David Warner trudges off. What an exit.

👍 0   👎 0   f 𝕐   ⦉ Share

3.4 overs

WICKET
Warner lbw Broad 2 (Aus 2-1)

Got him!

👍 514   👎 13   f 𝕐   ⦉ Share

Figure 5.8 BBC Sport Cricket web site extract.

Lofthouse, who reminds us of the time lapsed, reflecting on the shared sense of this being a short period through the use of the collective pronoun 'we'. She then offers a personal reflection on her emotions at this point, 'I can't take this', implying it is all too much excitement, thus adding to the sense of drama and engagement in the match by those in the commentary team as well as the fans following online. This is all part of the primary layer of narration, but we can also see the secondary layer being embedded in this text feed with Agnew's comment about sandpaper, which we will return to shortly.

The reproduction of live events, as we have seen in both oral and written commentary, is many-voiced. How is this managed visually online? We will look at part of the BBC Cricket commentary in more detail to explore this (Figure 5.9).

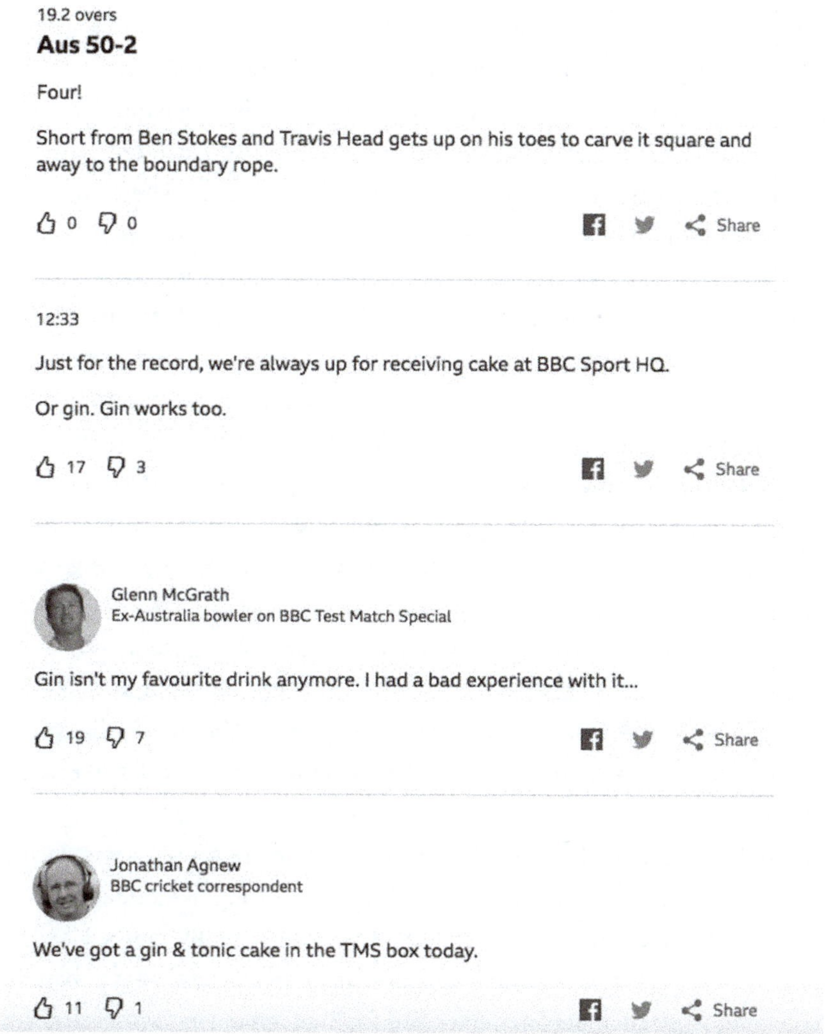

19.2 overs

Aus 50-2

Four!

Short from Ben Stokes and Travis Head gets up on his toes to carve it square and away to the boundary rope.

👍 0   👎 0   f   𝕐   ⤳ Share

12:33

Just for the record, we're always up for receiving cake at BBC Sport HQ.

Or gin. Gin works too.

👍 17   👎 3   f   𝕐   ⤳ Share

Glenn McGrath
Ex-Australia bowler on BBC Test Match Special

Gin isn't my favourite drink anymore. I had a bad experience with it...

👍 19   👎 7   f   𝕐   ⤳ Share

Jonathan Agnew
BBC cricket correspondent

We've got a gin & tonic cake in the TMS box today.

👍 11   👎 1   f   𝕐   ⤳ Share

Figure 5.9 BBC Sport Cricket web site extract.

Here we see the main contributor, Lofthouse, does not have her identity repeatedly flagged. In this screengrab, we can see that the top entry is the most recent and is Lofthouse's description score. At the top of this entry are the number of overs and balls bowled, the current score and then the relevant point of the entry: the Australian team have scored four runs. This is highlighted with the use of an exclamation point, before a brief description of the bowler's and batsman's actions. Below that, there is the opportunity to interact through approving or disapproving (the upturned and downward-turned thumbs), as well as widgets to link to Facebook and Twitter, and the capacity to copy the link. In order to understand the next entry (at 12.33), the reader needs to go back to entries to one contribution from a named reporter: in this case, Jonathan Agnew. This relates to cake, not cricket, and is part of the secondary narration Chovanec (2009) has discussed elsewhere. There is a long-running joke about cakes in the TMS commentary box, something that stretches back many decades, and so regular followers of test cricket would understand this reference. However, it is likely to be surreal to anyone who is not part of this in-group. This does, however, create a sense of community amongst followers of test cricket. That there is a virtual interaction between Agnew, McGrath and Lofthouse here is also important in creating this sense of comradery. The immediacy of this is highlighted in the use of present tense by all contributors to this pseudo-interaction, which fits with the more recent extract in this screengrab, where Lofthouse returns to commentating on the action.

The online reports, both on the web site and on Twitter, frequently report on the match crowd. For example, we can see a tweet from TMS, retweeted by BBC Sport (Figure 5.10), from the very beginning of the match that carries a large photo of a group of people waving squares of what looks like yellow paper.

It is only on reading the tweet that this begins to make sense, as it is clarified for us that these are England fans and that have brought sandpaper to the game. We are left to imply that this is what the photo actually shows. However, the relevance of this is only clear if readers are aware of the two-year ban that the opening Australian batsmen have had for 'ball tampering' with sandpaper in previous matches. The lack of any explanation beyond this enhances the

↻ BBC Sport Retweeted

Test Match Special ✓ @bbctms · 8m ⌄

The England fans have brought sandpaper to Edgbaston 😳

👉 bbc.in/2SXMqOJ

#bbccricket #ENGvAUS #Ashes

💬 19   ↻ 82   ♡ 318   ⬆

Figure 5.10 BBC Sport re-tweet of Test Match Special tweet.

sense of in-group community. The cricket fans who read this would know why this is relevant and so can make sense of the witty response of the co-present crowd to the return of two convicted cheaters.

Lofthouse continues to present a commentary of the events as they unfold on the field, but uses a conversational tone to ameliorate any formal properties of the commentary. For example:

Ah, James Anderson is back on the field!

Here, the properties of spoken language are clear, with the voiced expression of realization – 'Ah' – and the excitement of a returning player emphasized with the use of an exclamation point.

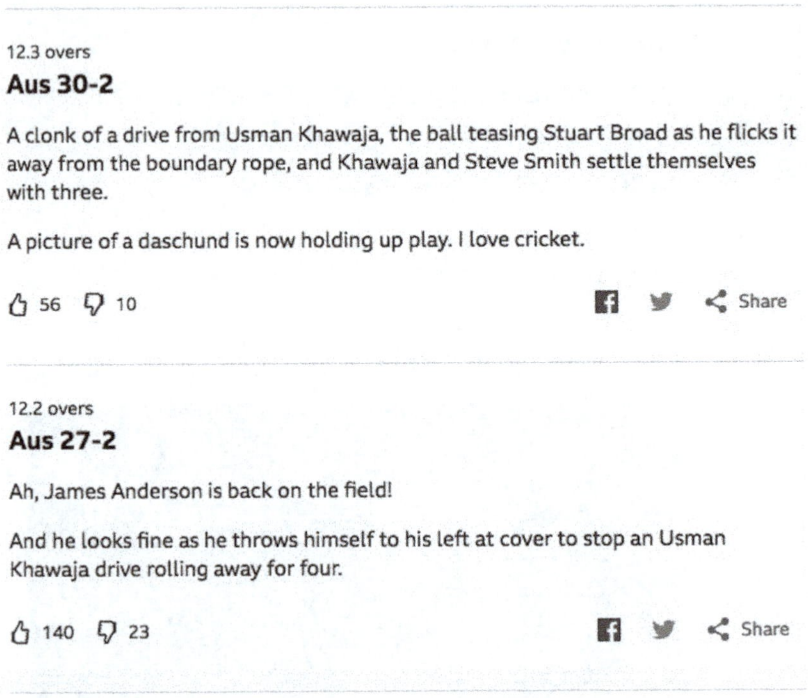

12.3 overs

Aus 30-2

A clonk of a drive from Usman Khawaja, the ball teasing Stuart Broad as he flicks it away from the boundary rope, and Khawaja and Steve Smith settle themselves with three.

A picture of a daschund is now holding up play. I love cricket.

👍 56   👎 10   f 🐦 ⤳ Share

12.2 overs

Aus 27-2

Ah, James Anderson is back on the field!

And he looks fine as he throws himself to his left at cover to stop an Usman Khawaja drive rolling away for four.

👍 140   👎 23   f 🐦 ⤳ Share

Figure 5.11 BBC Sport Cricket web site extract.

As Figure 5.11 shows, she follows this up with more details of Anderson's return to play, using a minor sentence to emphasize the informal, spontaneous nature of the commentary. The next entry from Lofthouse contains the emotive, informal expression of 'clonk' to add colour that the alternative of 'hit' fails to cover, in the same way as we saw in the use of 'punt' rather than 'kick' in the football commentary. This colour is further expanded as she then describes an interruption to play that is caused by a surreal image of daschund appearing in the ground (presumably interfering with the sight screen for the batsman, but not explained), this being something Lofthouse implies is part of the sometimes-surreal nature of cricket by her following sentence 'I love cricket'.

Whilst the commentary team do give the appearance of co-present involvement with one another online, what can we say of the involvement of online followers? Apart from the initial tweets in the build-up to the match

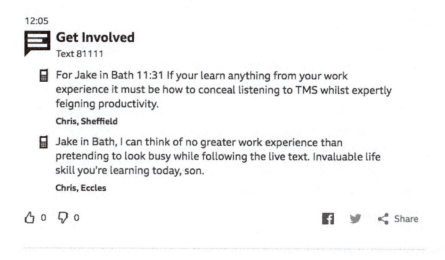

Figure 5.12 BBC Sport Cricket web site extract.

starting, there is little other direct address to the followers online. However, there is a text facility, and selected messages are reproduced in the web site (Figure 5.12). In this opening morning of the first Ashes text, one text in particular is used. This starts with the conventional 'text' logo of a squared-off message icon and the routine caption of 'Get Involved' in black print on a white background, and reproduced messages carry a tiny mobile phone icon. This helps to identify it in the rest of the live feed.

Much of this is part of the secondary narrative. One such example is reproduced from 'Jake in Bath' relates to his 'work experience' of trying to look productive for his boss whilst also trying to follow Test Match Special online. This leads to several other followers to text in with their support, such as 'Chris, Eccles' whose message is a direct address to Jake: 'I can think of no greater work experience than pretending to look busy while following the live text. Invaluable life skill you're learning today, son'. Here, Chris is addressing a wider audience about his own appreciation of cricket as followed with subterfuge (this is a concealed manoeuvre), then addresses Jake as a younger, less experienced comrade through the naming strategy of 'son'. Throughout the day, this developed into a theme that saw the 'Get Involved' caption change to 'How to follow the cricket at work', with frequent postings of helpful texts from other followers of the web site to help 'Jake in Bath' continue with this subterfuge. This example of Chovanec's secondary layer of narration is very common in online reporting, particularly of long-form sports such as cricket.

Both the BBC Sport web site and Twitter feed contain the voices of others who are not in the official commentary team nor members of the public who are loyally following the match. These voices come from others who use the relevant hashtags, or else are part of the wider community of sports journalists who are followed by the BBC Cricket team themselves.

For example, in this screengrab from the BBC Sport web site (Figure 5.13), there is an embedded tweet from Ben Jones, who is just described as 'From the press box', and his tweet provides additional historical information that is relevant to the recent live events. In keeping with the nature of his tweet's content, there is a use of past tense that is otherwise rarely found in the

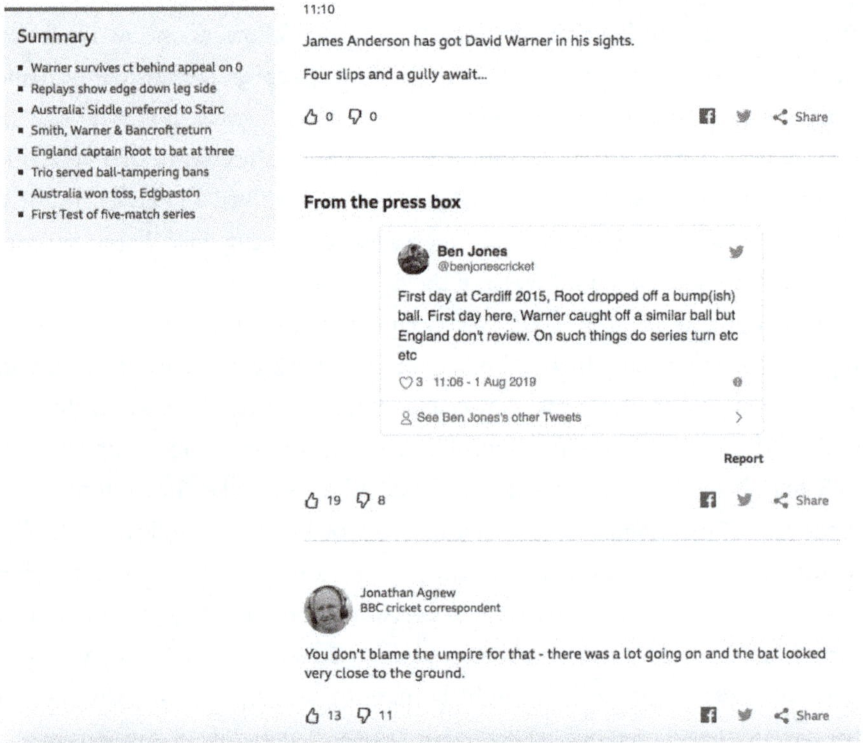

Summary

- Warner survives ct behind appeal on 0
- Replays show edge down leg side
- Australia: Siddle preferred to Starc
- Smith, Warner & Bancroft return
- England captain Root to bat at three
- Trio served ball-tampering bans
- Australia won toss, Edgbaston
- First Test of five-match series

11:10

James Anderson has got David Warner in his sights.

Four slips and a gully await...

👍 0   👎 0   f y < Share

From the press box

> **Ben Jones**
> @benjonescricket   y
>
> First day at Cardiff 2015, Root dropped off a bump(ish)
> ball. First day here, Warner caught off a similar ball but
> England don't review. On such things do series turn etc
> etc
>
> ♡3 11:06 - 1 Aug 2019   ⊕
>
> ⚇ See Ben Jones's other Tweets   >

                                                   Report

👍 19 👎 8   f y < Share

> **Jonathan Agnew**
> BBC cricket correspondent
>
> You don't blame the umpire for that - there was a lot going on and the bat looked
> very close to the ground.

👍 13 👎 11   f y < Share

Figure 5.13 BBC Sport Cricket web site extract.

commentaries of live events. The 'summary' box to the left of the page is relatively static, with just occasional updates on factual information. Even this is primarily written in present tense, with a shift to reflect yet-to-happen action where the main verb (go) is omitted and so the tense is ambiguously indicative, and past tense to reflect the events that have already happened in this match (Australia winning the toss, the three players who were banned for ball tampering, listed above as 'Smith, Warner & Bancroft').

Whilst the Twitter feed allows for comments and is relatively free for anyone to use, the web site is 'closed' as it is moderated. The absence of hashtags on the web site reflects this reduction of interactivity, nevertheless the use of colloquial language and quirky commentary help to make this web site more engaging in other ways.

In this way, a sense of community is being created whilst at the same time a live sporting event is being reported. This is an enhanced version of what Andrew Tolson (2006) and Stephanie Marriott (2007) argue about the difference between traditional TV and radio: that the TV sports viewer is given the position of ideal spectatorship (the best seat in the house), whereas the radio listener is offered a position with ideal spectators (the best seat with a like-minded community) (Tolson, 2006: 112). As Blake (2017) has explored in the wider context of the second screen, the technological affordances of apps and social media make this even more the case. This complex interweaving of static and dynamic text, social media and web pages, official and unofficial voices, requires a very high level of literacy from the reader. This is not least in the case of the BBC Sport web site, which, like other news outlet web sites reporting live events, has the most recent entry at the top, so essentially we have to start from the bottom and counter-intuitively read 'up' the page. That this is a convention of such 'live' web pages would appear to indicate that this is something that is not regarded as being a problem and does not detract us from our engagement with the text.

Sporting nationalism: inclusion and exclusion

So far, it has emerged how sports journalism is concerned in producing a timely account of unfolding events, while also conveying an appropriate emotional engagement. In this section, we look at how print sports journalism in particular situates this engagement with established discourses of shared affinity, particularly around national identity. Our discussion of the representation of national identity in sports journalism comes in two parts, one of which leads necessarily onto the other. In the first instance, we will look at the place of national identity at the centre of sports journalism, and the forms of discourse that are mobilized in order to secure and reproduce this shared sense of state belonging. Second, we will direct ourselves to the necessity of national identity to exclude non-nationals from its definitional boundaries (Anderson, 2006). In doing this, we will come to see how forms of framing and lexical choice conspire to define these 'others' in ways that simultaneously confect and emphasize their discord with the qualities associated with and treasured by the home nation.

Michael Billig (1995) emphasizes what he calls the 'banality' of our everyday relationship with national identity. As Higgins (2004: 634) describes it, 'Participation in a national collective is gently woven into routine daily practices, as well as habits of language.' In the circumstances of daily life, flags tend to stand unwaved rather than brandished aloft, and national belonging is as much as administrative as an emotional matter. In keeping with this lukewarm to simmering relationship with nation, the media provides one of the main settings in which the country moves in unison: watching the same weather forecast, buying similar newspapers, visiting web sites that contain the most mutually relevant news. However, where media turns to sport, and in particular the coverage of national sporting teams, a more emotionally affective relationship with the audience is secured by heating up the expression of national belonging, and foregrounding associated discourses and stereotypes.

If we look at the pronouns in this short editorial, we can see how there is a further emphasis on shared sense of community. In the first sentence, the collective pronoun 'we' creates an explicitly 'English' community ('we do not win much, we English'), but this is the English nation rather than the sports team. Whilst the actual act of winning is the responsibility of the sports players, the triumph is neatly glossed as being that of the nation by the joining of the players and spectators in the pronoun itself. Any distinction in the form of a reader who might not be English, or even interested in the achievements of a rugby team is disregarded by a nationalist discourse that collapses differences in class, gender, race and political ideology, and contains all within the same great national family.

The national media often symbolically convey the extent of unity by broadcasting footage of empty streets and shopping centres during major sporting events. We can see this from the next report (Table 5.8), published during the men's 2010 World Cup, when the *Daily Star* describes a sense of national anxiety and jubilation in its report of the England–Slovenia match:

Table 5.8 (*Daily Star*, 24 June 2010).

---

1. England's army of nervous fans finally had something to celebrate last night after the 1-0 victory that kept our World Cup dreams alive.
2. The whole country sprung back to life at 4.48pm after our nail-biting 1-0 win over minnows Slovenia in Port Elizabeth [...]
3. Earlier in the day England had ground to a halt, with major roads deserted and normally busy shopping centres empty.
4. Many schools finished lessons early so pupils and teachers could get home to watch the crucial match.
5. Other headteachers and business bosses across the country made special arrangements to enable fans to down tools and watch the game.
6. Sun-drenched music fans gathering for this weekend's Galstonbury rock festival even watched the drama unfold on a big screen.
7. Workers who did stay at their desks in the City of London managed to sneak a peak at the game on their computer screens, normally used for trading stocks and shares.

Even beyond the use of collective inclusive pronouns (e.g. paragraph 1: 'our World Cup hopes'; paragraph 2: 'our nail-biting 1–0 win'), this piece describes a sense of national unity that transcends age and social class. From school children to youthful music fans, shoppers to city workers: the span the presumed demographic of supporters glosses over the accompanying pictures of predominantly white men. However, as expressed through the language of the report, the 'whole country' has been watching the match, a point emphasized in paragraph 2 by the precision of the time at which the match ended this 'whole country sprung back to life'. All of this serves to reinforce the idea of an imagined community of millions which, Eric Hobsbawm (1990: 43) wryly notes, 'seems more real as a team of eleven named people'.

In terms of the experience of looking at and interpreting the newspaper, the headline is of crucial importance. Front and back page headlines (the back pages more associated with sports journalism) fulfil the dual function of arresting the attention of the casual passer-by and potential reader, while at the same time framing the subsequent reading of the story to come. Here, we are going to look at a series of headlines concerning the England men's football team's involvement in 2018. Since the newspapers themselves are reacting to events as they unfold, the most productive way of looking at the content of the headlines is to see how they develop in line with the progress of the tournament and the England team's fortunes: from the generation of shared excitement, through the expression of national unity and support, to reflections on the team's efforts.

> Let the three lions roar: England bring the nation together in quest for World Cup glory (*i*, page 1, 7–8 July 2018)

> Yeeesss!: Three lions mash Swedes to join last four; We're in the semi's for the first time in 28 years (*Sun on Sunday*, page 1, 8 July 2018)

> England gets a semi: nation in frenzy after three lions victory (*Daily Star*, page 1, 8 July 2018).

> Onwards: England march into semis (*Daily Telegraph*, page 1, 8 July 2018)

> My band of brothers: Harry's rallying call as England go for glory against Sweden at 3pm (*Daily Mirror*, page 1, 7 July 2018)

There headlines are clustered around the quarter final match between England and Sweden. Ordinarily, sports headlines would be concentrated on the back pages, but national participation in major tournaments occasionally requires that front pages be deployed for emphasis; which is the case with all four headlines featured here. We can see from the language used in the headlines that they are engaged in a number of tasks besides announcing the topic of the story and providing information on the event. First and most importantly, they are designed to convey the excitement of the occasion, in terms of both channelling the presumed engagement of the reader and establishing the tone of the writing itself. This is most explicit in the second headline's use of the extended declarative 'yeeesss', but is also apparent in the first headline's use of 'roar' to signal emotional expressiveness, and, in a rather more lurid manner, in the third headline's sexual punning in 'England gets a semi'. The third example, in particular, extends this shared pleasure in a shared joke with the readership on their presumed shared knowledge of sexual slang.

The next closely related task in which these headlines are engaged is the assertion of shared national community with the readership. In the first headline, 'the nation' is nominalized, albeit in a context in which its identity will be clear, and placed in a positive relationship with the team, expressed in synecdocheal terms as 'England'. A similar nominalization of 'England' occurs in the third headline, in which its collocation with 'frenzy' draws it within the shared excitement referred. But perhaps the most explicit example is the second headline, in which the inclusive pronoun 'we' includes the newspaper, readership and team in the successful progress to the next stage of the tournament.

As well as this, the sports headlines reproduce the association of this national identity with particular discourses and associated qualities. In order that the particular qualities of 'England' be set apart from other nations, all of whom have their own newspapers extolling their virtues, particular recognizable tropes are used. For example, the fifth extract from above produces an explicit reference to Henry V's battle speech in the eponymous Shakespeare play, extolling his 'band of brothers' to engage battle on England's behalf. We see parallel references from the following headlines, all from later in the tournament.

Land of hope and glory tonight (*Daily Express*, page 1, 11 July 2018)

England expects (*i*, page 1, 11 July 2018)

They're coming home, but every one's a hero (*The Sun*, page 1, 12 July 2018)

Situated on either side of the tie that the England team go on to lose and exit the tournament, these headlines are engaged in the production of a particular national mythology of battle and loss. We saw traces of this in the previous set we looked at, such that the first three call upon England's aggressive heraldic symbol and football team badge the 'lion', and the fourth calls upon a militaristic lexicon in 'onward' and 'England march'. With these headlines, we move into the realm of 'intertextuality', where national identity is expressed through the citation of tropes of shared significance, around which the readership will gather in recognition. The first headline quotes Elgar and Benson's patriotic song 'Land of hope and glory', commonly known in England through its association with the climatic night of the London-based classical music festival The Proms. The second headline cites a more explicitly martial expression of nationhood in Admiral Nelson's celebrated signal to his fleet at Trafalgar in 1805 that 'England expects that every man will do his duty', popularly cited since as an evocation of patriotic duty and a reminder of the accompanying expectations of victory. 'The third, however, cites a more contemporary popular cultural reference associated with English football, taking 'It's coming home' from the chorus of 'The Lightening Seeds' 1996 English football anthem 'Three lions'. The purpose of this rampant intertextuality is to call upon common and nationally specific points of reference in using language to foreground a convivial sense of belonging and common purpose between the journalist and the readership.

The possibilities for using the nation to claim a collective identity with the readership are perhaps at their most explicit on the front page of the *Daily Express* on 12 July, where the paper presumes to ventriloquize the national voice in a message to the national team 'We lived the dream … thank you England' (*Daily Express*, page 1, 12 July 2018). In this sense, and perhaps temporarily overlooking the militaristic connotations, summoning a national identity is a positive and collective experience, albeit subject to a particular shared memory and communal military experience. However, we began this section by noting that national identity had an exclusionary component, such that the supposed virtues of the home nation are routinely set in contrast with the shortcomings of other countries.

A number of scholars have argued that a more prejudicial use of nation is more readily associable with sports journalism because of its particular capacity for expansive description, subjective comment and localized forms of belonging. Hugh O'Donnell, for example, suggests that football coverage produces a taxonomy in which national and continental stereotypes are allowed to flourish: from the cool detach of the Scandinavians, to the surly cynicism of the Latin countries. We can see traces of this in the newspaper accounts of an England Women's World Cup tie with African nation Cameroon:

Cameroon's national team have been accused of 'shaming' women's football after they were knocked out by England in a last-16 clash at the World Cup that was marred with spitting, temper tantrums and claims of racism. England coach Phil Neville slammed the Cameroonian team for some of the worst behaviour he'd seen on a football pitch, saying it has left him 'completely and utterly ashamed' [...] On top of arguments about VAR, England's lionesses were spat on, elbowed in the face, and crunched in late tackles that left captain Steph Houghton needing treatment.

(*Daily Mail*, 23 June 2019)

At a superficial level, this is a straightforward account of poor and unsporting behaviour by one of the competing teams. In keeping with accepted journalistic practice, assessments of the conduct of the players, together with the 'shaming' claim, are outsourced to a witness; in this case the England team manager. Even then, a lurid list of charges is included in the unattributed text, including deliberate spitting and late tackles. The work of O'Donnell (1994) and Matheson (2005) suggests that far more latitude is available to describe performance as emotionally wrought and unsporting where the players are African, rather than European, with the assumption that such conduct is more readily associable with African football than may be expected in countries with which the readership are assumed to be more familiar. Another important component of this opposition is sustaining a positive outlook on the England players. While we have alluded to several examples before, but this is an opportune moment to highlight the importance of naming practices in ascribing meaning. The affectionate and empowering description of the 'lionesses' calls upon the same set of discourses as those associated with the men's team. In this case, it may be added that this is a nickname shared by the Cameroon team, who are known as 'the Indomitable Lions', with the Cameroonians enjoying the outward definitional advantage that stems from coming from a country in which lions are a natural part of the environment. However, here, and in similar coverage across other newspapers, the team is referred to mainly by their national designation. In terms of the projection of relationships with the competing teams, the mythical and emotive associations of the lion are reserved for the team most closely aligned with the presumed readership, thereby pursuing an emotional covenant between the journalistic text and the reader.

Conclusion

In this chapter, we have explored some of the linguistic skills and expressive potentials of sports journalism. But we have also highlighted some of the things we might look for in a critical appraisal of the language of sports commentary and coverage. We have seen that the sense of liveness is an important part of sports commentary, and how technology has enabled fans to get involved in the sense of community that sport engenders. We have explored how important this sense of community is, expressed both through the collaboration between the commentators and by means of the assumption of a shared sense of national identity and, occasionally, a sense of injustice. We have also looked at how this sense of national identity is a feature of sports reporting in the print media; how historical tropes and symbols associated with national belonging have become part of the coinage of popular journalism in expressing a national sense of togetherness and its association with the competitiveness of sport, and have seen something of how this attitude can draw upon broader and more invidious cultural assumptions.

Digital journalism

Introduction

This chapter will examine the influence of digital platforms on journalism; frequently perceived by journalists to be the main threats to the sanctity of journalism as we have come to know it. As we will see, in a way that often contrasts with broadcast or print, access to the platforms of delivery is comparatively open, enabling more fluid and dynamic forms of engagement from journalists, as well as the inclusion of a wider variety of voices. It certainly remains, however, that media institutions continue to press their advantage in the digital environment. In 2012, Natalie Fenton (2012: 558) charted the enthusiastic uptake of digital technologies by establishing news corporations, coupled with an emerging 'mutuality and interdependence' of content between digital and offline media platforms. The advantages are obvious, and one of the things that Fenton discusses is how online and digital systems offer capacity that would have been unthinkable in print or conventional broadcast media. Furthermore, as we will see here, digital journalism also lends itself to particular forms of engagement that have a dynamic relationship with the available affordances. By the end of the chapter, we will have established how digital journalism leans towards the multi-modal presentation of news, along with the development of new and informalized manners of engagement.

Dealing with the digital challenge

A great deal of the discussion concerning the shift to digital provision that goes on within the journalism profession concerns the impact on those financial models that have sustained the industry for much of the last two centuries. Partly, concerns have drawn on the dispersal of content onto phones, tablets and other forms of digital equipment, and the difficulties this presents in content control and monetization. As well as this, many of the journalists' misgivings stem from World Wide Web-inventor Tim Berners-Lee's vision of the internet as a means of providing and exchanging information in as free a manner as possible. For Berners-Lee (2000: 77), the role of the internet extends beyond the quantity and pliability of the data it is able to store, and is only fully realized when users are able to edit, manipulate and add to the material they find. While this as a vision has only been partially realized – and Wikipedia is a well-known example of its partial enactment – it is the internet that has certainly allowed us to take for granted immediate access to new information, and to assume easy access to the means to distribute information. To a certain extent, our voices in the form of tweets and podcasts can also be heard in ways that were previously unknown outside of the control of media authorities. We saw this in Chapter 5, where the live reporting of sports events is now routinely covered online by larger media organizations, frequently with the invocation to 'get involved' through sending comments via SMS or Twitter.

But what happens when we turn this towards the distribution of news? It is worth highlighting three opportunities for the development of journalism's conventions. The first we have already alluded to, which is the ease of access to news from an ever-greater variety of sources. As the means to produce web content is distributed more widely, professional news producers are encouraged to ensure that the material they produce is used more often and maintains an elevated status. Secondly, there are technical and informational advantages of the digital environment, where journalism has to adapt to deal with the immediacy and multi-modality of the online world. As Michael Bromley (2010: 31) predicted, the age of mass media has tended to move in the direction of 24/7 provision. While Bromley's tone is a pessimistic one, this does present a significantly greater capacity; offering journalists almost limitless amounts of space to fill with copy. Journalism also has increasing opportunities for emphasizing the sense of immediacy in a story; updates no longer have to wait until the next scheduled bulletin or paper edition, and rather can be added to a news web site on a minute-by-minute basis. Thirdly is the deprofessionalization of news provision. While there has been much important analysis of the rise of 'citizen journalism', we will look at the manner in which the professional performance associated with journalism has expanded to accommodate the conventions and affordances of digital platforms.

True to say, much more than the environment it is instrumental in shaping, the journalism industry has been called upon to the meet the challenge of a medium in which information, news and entertainment – the commodities in which journalism trades – have become freely available and subject to more rapid development. The aim here is to offer some ways to understand how the language of journalism is adapting to meet the various challenges presented. As we will see, the inclusion of non-professional voices has increased the diversity of language strategies on display, and in turn, has affected the linguistic style of professional journalists themselves.

We will begin our discussion of digital journalism with a brief exploration of how traditional news organizations have sought to engage a wider audience through web sites devoted to those news organizations.

Online news sites

The vast majority of news outlets now have an online presence, usually in the form of a specific web site that publishes stories in addition to those found in their print versions. When it comes to newspapers, the most visited English language site is that belonging to the *Daily Mail*. *Mailonline* was founded in 2003, and has expanded into Twitter, Snapchat and Facebook. At its peak, it attracted nearly 200 m visitors a month (Edge, 2015). This figure has decreased considerably since then, as other media outlets have copied the highly successful format of *Mailonline*, but in 2018, it was recorded as having more than 11.5 m daily readers, far outstripping its nearest rivals as well as dwarfing the circulation figures of around 1.5 m for the print version of the most popular paper in the UK, the *Metro* (which is distributed free of charge). The *Mailonline* also has aggressively marketed itself in the United States and in Australia, and the 'home' page offers readers the choice of tabs relating to their geographical preference. Such international pretensions are not limited to the *Mailonline*, as they are found in 'broadsheet' newspapers such as *The Guardian* and *The Times*. However, the *Mailonline* remains the most viewed and it is for this reason that it is worth exploring how the site is rendered readable.

If we return to Harcup and O'Neill's 2017 series of additional news values, the value of 'shareability' is undoubtedly one that is worth exploring further in this context. Cushion and Lewis's (2010) observations relating to the way in which rolling news is consumed – with rapid switching between channels requiring broadcasters to produce screen images that are clear and concise – we can see how the design of the *Mailonline* site is geared towards the casual user who is scrolling down the page. The page is punctuated by larger headlines and associated pictures that cover two-thirds of a width of the page, with two columns of stories below this on the same theme. These stories are all accompanied by pictures, and demonstrate the aim made from the start that pictures would be the focus of the web site to attract more users.

The third column on the page is the infamous 'sidebar of shame'. This is a vertical column at the right side of the screen, picture-orientated with a short summary rather than headline. Its nickname refers to the fact that it is often the area where 'papped' photos of off-guard celebrities appear, their unpolished appearance often being the focus of the story. We can see examples of this in the illustration below (Figure 6.1), and which we discussed in more detail in the Newspapers chapter.

What we can see from these typical captions is that each starts with the name of the celebrity about whom the story will be developed. This makes the story more searchable by the casual scroller. Thus even with the least identifiable image, often grabbed snaps rather than consciously posed, the identity of the celebrity is clear. Unlike headlines, there is a little attempt at playful language, nor a systematic avoidance of function words. Where function words are omitted, these are infrequent and they tend to be personal pronouns: 'Sophie Turner flashes HER toned stomach', or determiners: 'Megan Fox puts on a stylish display in A strapless black jumpsuit'.

▶ **Sophie Turner flashes toned stomach and lean legs during outing with Joe Jonas in NYC after solo lunch dates**
Spotted wearing a crop top and denim shorts

▶ **Gigi Hadid and rumored beau Tyler Cameron enjoy dinner date with Serena Williams and friends in NYC**
Night out

▶ **Megan Fox puts on a stylish display in strapless black jumpsuit as she attends Seoul photocall for Battle of Jangsari**
Stunning

▶ **Is Chanel Iman pregnant? Model steps out with burgeoning belly on outing with daughter**
Looked to be expecting baby number two

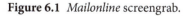

Figure 6.1 *Mailonline* screengrab.

We can also see the smaller text, in black print rather than blue (which semiotically indicates the presence of a hyperlink), is smaller but essentially offers an opinion about the point of view the reader should take: Sophie Turner is 'wearing a crop top and denim shorts', something that is clear from the associated photograph, but highlighted for us in this lengthy verb phrase. We are directed towards an opinion regarding Megan Fox: 'stunning', and more contextual information about Chanel Iman in yet another verb phrase: 'looked to be expecting baby number two'. Essentially, the combination of photo and tantalizing image renders the story as clickbait, thus illustrating Harcup and O'Neill's (2017) point about shareability. Once users click on the hyperlink, they arrive at the expanded version of the story, often with few words but a large number of pictures, and the option of sharing the story online in other forms of social media through prominent widgets under the main headline.

It is not only print media outlets that have online sites: broadcasters also have similar sites where their news stories are presented as hyperlinks to videos as well as written versions of the reports, as we have already seen. If we look at the web site for CNN (Figure 6.2), one of the first things we can notice is that there are fewer pictures than we find on *Mailonline*. However, the traditional three-column format is one that is replicated. There is a similar attempt at

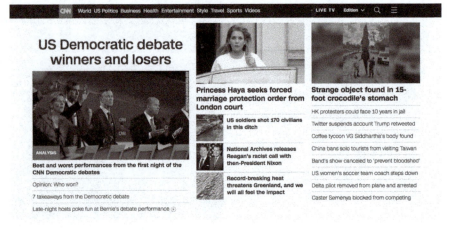

Figure 6.2 CNN website.

tantalizing headlines to be clicked: the main story relates to Democratic party debates and is a grading of 'best and worst performances', and '7 takeaways'. These are akin to the listicles that make a story shareable through clickbait strategies. The middle column is devoted to more sensational stories. The main story here refers to 'forced marriage', whilst the other three stories rely on assumptions of readers. For example, the US focus of the broadcaster has a presupposition of pride in the military that is challenged by the headline declaring US soldiers may have been guilty of war crimes by the mention of '170 civilians' and 'ditch'. The historical racism in politics is given currency through a story about the National Archive, which is rendered current through the use of the present tense verb 'releases'. The third story is not local, in that it refers to a distant country, but is rendered relevant through the use of the collective pronoun 'we'.

The third column, to the far right of the page, like the *Mailonline*'s sidebar, is shorter and more succinct, but here it is restricting its headlines to just one line and so they appear as bullet listing. The restricted space means that there is a large amount of lexical and grammatical omission, particularly through abbreviations and omission of function words. For example, Hong Kong is reduced to 'HK', and Delta Airlines to just 'Delta'. Elsewhere, the name of the band whose show has been cancelled is omitted, as the main point of the story is not the band, but the sensationalization of the threat of 'bloodshed'. In this way, users of the site are treated as sharing a common understanding of the cultural and political context of the stories who need no further explanation as to why a story would be of interest.

Twitter: promotion and projection

News outlets generally have an online Twitter account, linked to their main web site. One of the purposes of these Twitter accounts is to 'attract attention online' (Hong, 2012: 69), by directing readers to the main site by offering tantalizing or pithy summaries of the main stories. Often, the same linguistic strategies as we found in headlines are used here: expanded nouns as headwords; omission of function words; short declarative statements. In this section, we will explore how journalism has used Twitter to produce these traditional elements of print media, while also embracing and being shaped by the developments in technology that Twitter has brought.

In order that this connection between the tweet and the main story be a straightforward one, hyperlinks can be embedded into individual tweets. These hyperlinks can be in the form of conventional links to other web sites, particularly the specific new outlet's own main web site. However, they can also be links to other relevant Twitter accounts, whereby the Twitter handle can act as a tagging device or shorthand summary of a longer name, in a manner that includes the other user in the conversation:

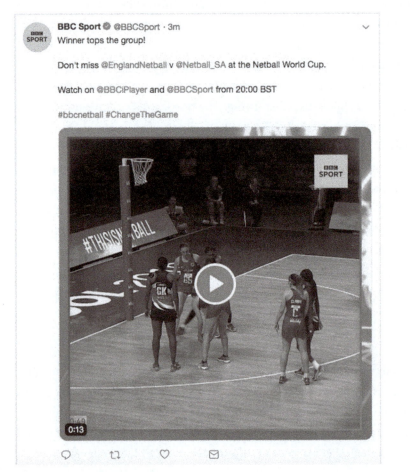

Figure 6.3 BBC Sport tweet.

In this tweet (Figure 6.3) from *BBC Sport*, the two competing teams are identified solely by their Twitter handles. This makes readability of the text rather difficult, as it supposes that the reader will know to whom the Twitter handle relates. Whilst this is clear in the case of @EnglandNetball, it is less straightforward with the South African team's handle where the name of the country is abbreviated to SA. Such uncertainties are often occasioned by the obligation for a Twitter handle to be unique, which frequently produces alpha-numeric and punctuation combinations that are less literal than the England Netball, of which the @Netball_SA handle is an example. This may be partially resolved for online users choosing to engage with the Twitter feed as the handles appear in blue text, as the interface on larger devices prompts the description of the Twitter account to appear when the cursor hovers over the hyperlink. Further hyperlinks are found in the embedded link to a short video of the teams in action, which itself provides a still image to illustrate the tweet.

The tweet also includes hashtags #bbcnetball #ChangeTheGame. We can see in these two hashtags how different graphological strategies are necessary. The first hashtag, #bbcnetball comprises the conventional and well-known abbreviation BBC, and this is followed immediately by the name of the sport. The readability of the hashtag is only possible because of the pre-existing familiarity of the BBC abbreviation, but it means that the hashtag is understandable without much effort on the part of the reader. The second hashtag comprises three words, and relates to a slogan that was introduced by BBC Sport in the summer of 2019 to relate to the promotion of women's sport, specifically in the case of female athletes. The readability of this particular hashtag is rendered possible by the word boundaries being marked by initial capitals.

Hashtags are a useful way for social media users to make their postings searchable. Sites such as Twitter and Instagram allow for the quick search of these features, thus allowing common interests to be shared between users who may not already 'follow' each other. In this case, the hashtags are positioned at the end of the tweet. In other tweets, the hashtags actually form part of the utterance. For example, as in Figure 6.4:

Figure 6.4 BBC Sport tweet.

Nathan Rambukkana (2015: 2) stresses the dynamic and still-ongoing character of such hashtags and the possibilities of their use, ranging from promotional to the 'linking or constituting particular publics'. In the example above, we can see this flexibility of use in terms of how the hashtag contributes to the coherence of the tweet. The hashtag #ChampionsLeague works coherently as part of the sentence's structure, both specifying the competitive context of the match and enabling users with a general interest in the Champions League to locate the tweet. On the other hand, the #bbcfootball hashtag sits above the image of Klopp in the lower part of the tweet, and operates more in the projection of a community of interest around BBC football coverage, to which the tweet contributes. Thus, we can see immediately that hashtags are being used in two different ways: to make the tweet more searchable, while claiming the tweet's place in a broader communicative environment.

In the BBC Sport tweet, we also see an example of the convention of embedding a hyperlink to the main web site. It is heralded as 'in full', which carries the implicature that the story as it appears in the tweet is not the complete story. Here, the story is summarized briefly as 'Jurgen Klopp says he would "100%" support attempts to bring a #ChampionsLeague final to Murraryfield'. The link between Klopp – at this time manager of Liverpool FC, and what happens to be the national Scottish rugby stadium in Edinburgh is not offered any context to make it more explicit. So the tantalizing lack of information, coupled with the high-profile sporting event of the Champions League football tournament, is intended to draw the reader into clicking on the hyperlink for more details. That this is intended to be a positive story is indicated by the accompanying photo of Klopp, raising his arm in acknowledgement whilst being surrounded by Liverpool players applauding.

The perils of the short-form journalism of Twitter can sometimes lead to misunderstandings or a general lack of clarity. Another tweet from BBC Sport (Figure 6.5) shows how the semantic properties of some utterances, including the conventions of Twitter, include the possibility of misinterpretation:

BBC Sport ✔ @BBCSport · 13m   ⌄
Hearts owner Ann Budge has called on supporters to expose those responsible for the "disappointing" scenes during Wednesday's Edinburgh derby.

Hibs' manager was struck by a coin and Hearts' goalkeeper was hit by a fan.

Read bbc.in/2DeUqWx

Figure 6.5 BBC Sport tweet.

Here, the second sentence has the parallel structure of 'struck by' and 'hit by'. There is a resultant implied unity between 'coin' and 'fan' which is open to misunderstanding by virtue of the noun 'fan' having several different meanings in English. We have to shift from the lack of a human agent in the first part (a coin does not move on its own: it must have had someone actually throw it, therefore additional human agency is invisible), to the actual human agent – the fan, or supporter – being visible in the second part. If we do not make this shift, then the fan, like the coin, may be assumed to be inanimate object, in this case a small hand-held object for cooling the face. This renders the potential for serious physical assault more comedic than the journalist would have intended.

Twitter: real-time immediacy

Twitter is also used in journalism to report events in real-time. This is particularly useful in the case of sporting events.

Immediacy is also relevant in the case of breaking news stories. Many newspapers will have Twitter accounts that carry 'breaking news' bulletins that can be linked to mobile phone settings to allow for automatic notifications on the lock screen. These tweets would be linked to the main account of the news outlet. However, they can also be further linked to reporting by individual journalists. For example, the following tweet (Figure 6.6) by the *Los Angeles Times* newspaper relates to a breaking story about a shooting at a festival in California.

The news outlet's main site has retweeted one tweet by the LA City Editor of the *LA Times*, Hector Becerra. This tweet has embedded in it a tweet by an on-the-scene *LA Times* journalist, Laura J. Nelson, who has tweeted a short update on her status: she is 'en route to Gilroy' (Gilroy is about an hour-and-a-half's drive away from central LA). There is no further

ti   Los Angeles Times Retweeted

Hector Becerra ✔ @hbecerraLATimes · 7h

Follow Laura and @LATvives who are traveling north for the #GilroyGarlicFestivalshooting @latimes

> 🔘 **Laura J. Nelson** 🔫 ✔ @laura_nelson · 7h
> En route to Gilroy
> Show this thread

◯ 1   ti 18   ♡ 21   ⬆

Figure 6.6 LA Times tweet.

information in this tweet, but Becerra's tweet contextualizes it using the hashtag #GilroyGarlicFestivalshooting. Becerra's tweet carries the directive to 'follow' Laura, then the handle of a further *LA Times* journalist whose name is obscured by their chosen Twitter name. In the lexicon of Twitter, this enjoins the reader to click on colleagues' accounts to 'follow' their tweets. In terms of contemporary news practice, the assumption behind this is that these journalists are in a position to offer first-hand accounts of developments (Peters, 2001). The suggestion to follow these journalists on Twitter thereby creates a sense of urgency and immediacy.

In practical terms, the utility of this is limited as the accounts of both of these named journalists reveal little activity relating to reporting of the shooting. Nelson has only one more tweet, which comments on her sadness of reporting on another mass shooting, but free of additional information about this particular tragedy. For such information, readers need to sustain their engagement with the main *LA Times* Twitter feed which retweets various sources of information, such as local news reports, police reports and eye witness accounts, with limited input from the news organization itself. Nonetheless, while we see the limits of this practice, the inherent mobility of Twitter demands a style informed by immediacy and the presence of experiential journalism.

Journalists using Twitter to generate stories

Twitter is also used to generate stories. Sometimes this is explicitly on the part of the news outlet, using its official Twitter handle. In other cases, there are individual journalists who tweet appeals for stories, where their tweets will often be retweeted by the main news outlet. Sarah Marsh, acting as a journalist at *The Guardian*, frequently uses Twitter to ask people to get in touch with her regarding specific stories. Here are two of her tweets (Figures 6.7 and 6.8) which have been retweeted by *The Guardian*, both relating to the same story, which is about a music festival (Boardmasters) being cancelled in anticipation of bad weather.

Her own agency is foregrounded here. In the first tweet (Figure 6.7), she uses first person pronouns – 'I am going to be in Newquay ...' before

⟲ The Guardian Retweeted

Sarah Marsh ✔ @sloumarsh · 2h

I am going to be in Newquay today to speak to people about alternative plans now #boardmasters2019 has been cancelled. Please get in touch to be interviewed: sarah.marsh@theguardian.com or tweet me. #boardmasterscancelled

💬 5   ⟲ 3   ♡ 11   ⬆

Figure 6.7

⟲ The Guardian Retweeted

Sarah Marsh ✔ @sloumarsh · 1h

Anyone going to Newquay regardless of #boardmasters2019 being cancelled? Email me to let me know your plans: sarah.marsh@theguardian.com

💬 2   ⟲ 2   ♡ 7   ⬆

Figure 6.8

the main reason for her tweet, an appeal for contributors. This is done by employing politeness markers that recognize social distance, using 'please' to acknowledge social distance and obligation. In contrast, her second tweet (Figure 6.8) is more informal. There is an inclusive 'anyone' to whom the tweet is addressed where they are presented as devil-may-care in going to a festival that they would know has been cancelled (they are 'regardless'). This accords the subjects of the tweet with a carefree disregard for the weather. In both tweets, there is an assumption of there being alternative arrangements, glossed informally as 'plans'. In the second tweet, Marsh uses the second person pronoun to directly address the adventurous festival-goers. Thus, we see here a projection of the individual over journalistic persona, combined with the use of a variety of politeness tactics in inviting the readers to engage in interpersonal correspondence. Against this, here are still formal qualities to underpin the professional effectiveness of the tweets: the journalist uses the hashtag #boardmasters2019 to make her tweet more searchable, and the tweet is finished with a work email address, which is a hyperlink and thus would allow for ease of communication for those who have a smartphone.

This is not always the case. As mentioned above, the *New York Times* tends to appeal for contributions via its central Twitter account rather than that of a named journalist. For example, in reporting on the rise in knife crime in London in 2018, the news outlet tweeted: 'Have you experienced a petty crime in London? Click to tell us your story. (Your submission may be selected for publication.)' (Figure 6.9).

Here, there is a direct question being asked, using second person pronouns. The second sentence is an imperative, contrasting with Marsh's invitation. The news outlet refers to itself in the collective first person pronoun. This is a much more informal approach than Marsh's, but lacks the individual voice of the journalist. The final sentence in this tweet is located in parenthesis. As we saw in the case of parenthesis in magazines earlier, this can be used as a friendly aside. However, here it is being used in place of legal small print, as we saw in the case of the BBC Sport tweet in the previous chapter. The tweet has embedded in it the full story as found on the main web site, but with

Figure 6.9

the added information of a colour photo of a group of British police officers walking in line along a residential street (to British readers, this picture would indicate crowd control policing rather than crime fighting, signalled by the hi-vis jackets officers wear in such contexts). Under this picture, the text of the main tweet is repeated in bold, but with the added detail that contextualizes the story: 'As the city's level of violent crime rises, help us understand how the London police are responding to minor property crimes'. There is an odd juxtaposition of 'violent crime' and 'minor crime'. This tension between serious and petty quickly led to the UK followers of the *New York Times* Twitter account responding with parody 'crimes' that, within a very short space of time, had become a viral event. The responses were entirely humorous, generally poking fun at British sensibilities and London cultural norms in particular. More than eleven thousand responses were recorded within twenty-four hours, and not one of them was helpful to the *New York Times*' intended story. However, the parodying of the original tweet made it onto the national news in the UK, and became a story in its own right. What we see now is a shift from the individual journalist requesting story generation from twitter users, to a news institution framing an established story and eliciting reaction, albeit with unintended consequences, as the following tweets (Table 6.1) show:

Table 6.1 Extracts of responses to *New York Times* tweet.

Mike Stuchberry
Replying to @nytimes
I once paid for a bus with my phone and held up the queue for fifteen seconds. #pettycrime

Michael Strachan
Replying to @nytimes
A London cabby once refused to accept my Clydesdale Bank ten pound note, even after a lengthy and highly educational explanation as to the difference between legal tender and acceptable currency.

Jen
Replying to @nytimes
I watched somebody accidentally walk into a lamppost and they didn't apologise to it. As I live and breath! #pettycrime

Ben Ashton
Replying to @nytimes
Naiively accompanied colleagues for drinks after work to Camden. Pub charging ten quid a pint. Daylight robbery! #pettycrime

As we can see from these examples, several users have rendered their sardonic responses more searchable through the use of the #pettycrimes hashtag. However, as we noted above, the hashtag has another function aside from searchability: it is also inclusive. In a manner that displays both the power of the hashtag and the critical capacity of the readers, #pettycrimes has functioned 'to coordinate public discussion and informal-sharing on news and political topics' (Bruns and Burgess, 2015: 17).

Media organizations' use of social media to generate stories is one way in which non-professionals are able to have a voice in news media. This is a form of what is known as 'citizen journalism', which we will explore in more detail now.

Citizen journalism: practices and identities

We began the chapter by noting that a benefit of online is the potentially limitless amount of space. For news organizations, this is at once an advantage and a disadvantage. On the one hand, any quantity of stories, any amount of explanatory information can be provided through links to online videos, podcasts and pages of text. On the other hand, with this extra capacity comes the expectation and responsibility to provide more material than before. Thurman (2008) looks at the shift towards drawing upon user-generated content. Often, this involves users being invited to submit material to supplement or illustrate the story. As we saw in our discussion of online sports reporting, the BBC Sport media presence encouraged users to 'Get Inspired', with their words being reproduced in blogs and tweets. However, the use of citizen-generated content extends beyond the occasional contribution from a normally acquiescent individual, and some way outside of the control of traditional news institutions.

Citizen journalists are those who seek to intervene as journalists, but from outside of a professional/institutional context. Mark Glaser (2012: 478) defines the citizen journalist as someone who 'without journalism training can use the tools of modern technology and the global distribution of the Internet to create, augment or fact-check media on their own or in collaboration with others'. Yet, Glaser acknowledges some considerable overlap between citizen and mainstream, professional journalists. For example, using blogs and other social media, professional journalists can temporarily occupy those realms that have come to be associated with citizen journalism, occasionally engaging the audience in a slightly different tone and marking their input as more 'personal' (commonly, their signature lines include a disclaimer that their views are their own, and not their employers'). However, the authority of the journalist still draws upon conventional resources, of the sort illustrated by the following by-line:

Figure 6.10

Figure 6.10 shows a by-line for *Scottish Sun* sports opinion columnist Davie Provan. This follows a number of visual and linguistic conventions that lay claim to institutional, professional authority. Most striking is the recurrent house design of the by-line, framing the stern expression of a writer embodying his sombre commitment to truth and duty. This mood of journalistic focus is also expressed in the alliterative slogan 'Frank and Fearless', which combines earnestness with the reputational capital accumulated by regular and prolonged visibility. Although the distribution of such authority is more democratized than a newspaper column, when attached to a Twitter handle, such professional status is associated with the 'blue tick' mark of authentication.

This notion of conventional journalistic authority and how it relates to Twitter is important for thinking about how journalism is publicized and develops. In terms of the implications of digital platforms as they develop, broadcast, newspaper and sports journalists in particular maintain their own Twitter accounts, where, on the one hand, they enjoy the same capacity and expressive latitude as other users (Hermida, 2009: 299), but where they can continue to exploit the professional and reputational capital gathered on other platforms. As we will go on to explore later it this chapter, podcasts are the most recent development in digital journalism, and demonstrate this blend of professional convention and performance of informality. In terms of the lesson for the influence of the digital realm, these have developed out of the popularity of 'citizen journalist' podcasts, where the conversational style they adopt has become a convention of the medium.

Aside from these institutional forays into social media, what purpose does citizen journalism serve? Glaser notes that citizen journalism is driven by the conviction that more knowledge and a greater variety of perspectives are available to the many members of the audience than can be gathered by the institutions of journalism or certainly by the individuals working there. In Fenton's (2012: 559) terms, citizen journalism introduces a greater degree of 'multiplicity and polycentrality' to news, widening the scope of the content beyond that favoured by the established news centres. In addition to the introduction of diversity, there is also an increased reach in the collective powers of journalistic surveillance. That is to say, with the exception of a pre-arranged press conference, those positioned around a newsworthy event are more likely to be 'ordinary' citizens going about their daily tasks than professional journalists. Many of these citizens now have the technology to record, tweet and upload images of what they find, or post unedited accounts of their experiences to a worldwide audience.

Far from being a limitation on the utility of non-professional images, this is a discourse that contributes to the overall aura of online news: that it is immediate, vital, visceral; with the ever-present danger of undue haste to make public error and misinterpretation. In keeping with this, those images most attuned to the mood of citizen journalism are those that explicitly amateurish in their manner. Free of the sorts of editorial restraint described by Thurman (2008: 144), the aura of citizen-input resides in its uncultured, unschooled style. Low-resolution video taken with an unsteady hand, while some way short of professional production standards, is the marker of authenticity in non-professional, citizen-driven content. A convention has emerged whereby such images – both static and video – when used by traditional media are framed by a blurred extension of the original to mark it apart from the clear-cut images of the professional producers (see the screengrab of CNN's web site for an example of this in Figure 6.2).

In her discussion of a new immediacy of journalistic transmission, Angela Phillips (2012) highlights another way in which the inherent immediacy of such citizen journalism environments as social media impacts upon the journalistic mainstream: that of setting the terms of conversation, and subsequent coverage. The # hashtag is a way of flagging the salient word or phrase in a Twitter message. The use of a hashtag attached to a term enables Twitter users to search for a word. In addition to this, when a particular topic is hashtagged by a substantial portion of users within a short period, it is flagged by Twitter as 'trending' and so becomes an item of common currency amongst users. The sudden rise of an item to public prominence in this way falls within the metaphor of 'going viral', and the potential to set the public agenda in this way is as much within the power of charities, NGOs, pressure groups and ordinary citizens as it is with journalists. Where a searchable word or phrase or hashtag 'goes viral', it can become a media story in its own right, with screengrabs of tweets illustrating a story of how citizens in the guise of viewers or supporters have 'taken to Twitter' to raise their objections. 'Taken to Twitter' stories are frequently found in online versions of newspapers, where the screengrabs of the relevant tweets provide illustration of the report, which is most often reflecting the news value of negativity. Twitter therefore distributes the potential for agenda-setting more widely than the traditional journalistic platforms and professional actors. Hashtags are not only used to make something searchable (Kroon 2017), but offer a possible opportunity for interaction, as we saw in our discussion of online sports reporting and will go on to explore in more detail later in this chapter.

Online journalism and authorship: branding

In the chapter on broadcast journalism, we discussed the importance of understanding journalism as a particular form of personalized testimony, and in the section above we look at just one example of how particular types of persona are established within a professionalized setting. In a context in which professional journalists, citizen journalists and interested bystanders jostle on a shared platform, it will be revealing to discuss the developing language of authorship and identity. Saska Saarkoski (2012) suggests a campaign of 'branding' individuals as reputable authorities; various sorts of agents all perceived as 'valued content producers' (Saarkoski, 2012: 4) with varying qualities of experience, sincerity, expertise, pithiness of expression, professionalism and institutional support. The notion of branding has challenges as well as benefits, and Alan Rusbridger (2018: 279) warns of 'the trophy newspaper' as a legacy brand for attracting advertisers and packaging giving the sheen of legitimacy to substandard content across digital platforms. This is the challenging environment into which the journalist as 'brand' is judged, negotiating a cultural antipathy towards 'celebrity journalists' (Saarkoski, 2012: 48) against the professional imperative to gather reputational capital and make content stand out.

In keeping with suggestions of branding, and whether they develop deliberately or implicitly, the popularization of blogs and sites like Twitter is consistent with a continuing authorial regime in news and comment. And as Mary Angela Block (2012) argues as she shows how citizen journalists work at lending 'authority' to their content, this applies as much to individuals as to news corporations. Individuals in a position to tweet from news hot spots or with inside information in politics or sport can accumulate an archive of work and establish some measure of truth-telling status. The opportunity to use media platforms to bear what John Durham Peters (2001) calls a particular kind of 'witness' to an event is now as widespread as digital camera or mobile phone ownership allows. As Stuart Allan (2010: 219) points out, many of the most significant examples of citizen journalism do not come from those setting out to establish a reputation. Usually, the most compelling examples come from those 'in the wrong place at the wrong time' and able to report authoritatively on a scenario they happen to inhabit. How, then, are these developments likely to become apparent at the level of representation? One prominent strategy for marking out citizen journalism and laying claim to its benefits is to use language to assert distance from a professional context, as this Twitter header from a well-known UK citizen journalist illustrates (Figure 6.11):

Figure 6.11

We have talked elsewhere about an emphasis on informal language, and here we see an ironic shift from a professional-institutional to a conversational register in the qualifier 'mainly', surrendering any professional-appropriate claims to consistency. Claiming the insult 'Stooge', the header then ventriloquizes a number of the accusations made against their claim to truth and neutrality, implicitly displaying them as outlandish and contradictory. Also in an ironic mode, the authority of the writer is surrendered through a direct address to the hostile reader ('I can fix that for you').

A multi-modal approach to digital journalism therefore demands attention to the visual and linguistic strategies used to anchor the brand of the individual source, author, journalist or news organization, or the tactics used to assert their independent, non-professional credentials. In other words, we should look at the means and strategies deployed by authors of whatever type to emphasize their particular credentials and warrant to speak.

In a way that cuts across citizen journalism from non-professionals and trained journalists using social media such as podcasts and Twitter, it is therefore worthwhile exploring citizen journalism as a particular form of activity that places an emphasis on certain types of linguistic engagement. This has the advantage of offering some respite from the debate over whether citizen 'journalism' amounts to an abuse of a pseudo-professionalized designation (Glaser, 2012: 581). There may be scope for looking at citizen journalism as a means of providing statement and comment, but without laying claim to professional insight, or the obligations of the trained and accredited news provider. As a form of practice that can be available to professional journalists, given the appropriate symbolic concessions, citizen journalism thus emerges as the performance of a relatively unconstrained form of discursive power, with less emphasis on the practices of objectivity, detachment and balance.

We will finish our discussion of digital media with a brief exploration of the most recent journalistic development: the podcast. Emerging from non-professional sources, these have been adopted as a medium by news organizations but the linguistic features, as we shall see, carry traces of this non-professional, citizen journalist communicative strategy.

Journalism on the go: podcasts

Podcasts are one of the more recent developments in online technology that have had an impact on journalism. Janet Kunert and Neil Thurman (2019: 766) identify podcasts as important vehicles for the personalization of journalism, and show a particular acceleration in their use since 2016, particularly in publications that place an emphasis on expertise, such as the *Financial Times* of London and the *Wall Street Journal* in New York. The portmanteau noun 'podcast' comprises the brand name 'iPod' and 'broadcast', first appearing in 2004 (in an article by *The Guardian* journalist Ben Hammersley) to describe a digital audio file which can be downloaded and listened to at leisure. This means that, unlike many other forms of online journalistic content, podcasts can be listened to at a time that suits the consumer and without access to Wi-Fi (Burns and Matthews, 2018). Accordingly, podcasts are seen as more audience-focused than other forms of journalistic production. They are also usually episodic in nature, and listeners can choose to subscribe to a series, setting up an arrangement in which the podcast will be automatically 'dropped' into their mobile phone or tablet.

In terms of genre and purpose, podcasts generally fall into one of three categories:

1. Entertainment, such as fictional works, music-related content.
2. Extensions of existing broadcasts, such as expanded interviews found in traditional media.
3. News and current affairs, where journalists and others present documentaries or thematic news stories.

It is the third of these that we will explore in more detail.

Major news outlets are devoting huge resources to podcasting. For example, in the UK, in 2018 the BBC appointed its first Commissioning Editor for Podcasts. Commissioned content is designed to be different in tone and form to traditional broadcasts, and, pursuing the notion of the expert voice identified above, include exclusive content such as *Political Thinking* with BBC political editor Nick Robinson and *Brexitcast* (which we will look at below). In the United States too, CNN has also developed an extensive podcast catalogue, including *The Daily DC* and *CNN News Briefing*, a daily three-minute summary of the news headlines. Podcasting also provides a platform for independent journalists who mobilize the capacity for longer form journalism (Burns and Matthews, 2018), particularly those specializing in online investigation, such as *Bellingcat*.

Podcasting in action: informed while informal

We have noted that the context for consumption of podcasts is the convenience of the listener, without the burdensome imposition of broadcasting schedules. In addition, we have emphasized their design for downloading and storage, to be listened to free of the constraints of Wi-Fi or a data signal. Allied to the personalized character of the content, these are conditions of production and consumption suited to a more generally relaxed style. If we look at one such broadcast from the BBC catalogue, we can explore how the interactional style emerges as markedly less formal than we would expect in traditional broadcasting.

We will look at the example of *Brexitcast*, which is a half-hour weekly podcast featuring BBC journalists Katya Adler (Europe Editor), Adam Fleming (Europe Correspondent), Laura Kuenssberg (Political Editor), and from Chris Mason (Political Correspondent). In May 2019, it was the recipient of the Listeners' Choice Award at the British Podcast Awards, and so is a successful example of its type. Although packaged as a weekly release, there are additional episodes recorded to coincide with significant events on an ad hoc basis (such broadcasts are mischievously prefaced with reference to a 'klaxon', meaning a brash signal). This particular episode coincides with the start of the summer recess of the UK parliament, and so this episode is subtitled 'Out of office',

Table 6.2

AF	Hello Brexitcasters (.) it's Adam here (.) and welcome to your (.) third	1
	helping of Brexistcast this week (.) though we're recording this on (.)	
	Thursday late afternoon so it feels like a (.) normal (.) chilled out (.)	
	Brexitcast (.) in a week that has been (.) far from normal or (.) chilled (.) out	
	(.) now Laura's going to be in the studio (.) we're going to be joined by (.) a	5
	guest (.) as you know (.) Chris is off on leave and Katya is in the Bavarian	
	mountains (.) I think today she's on a (.) nine hour car journey with her kids	
	(h.) good luck with that one (.) and actually this could potentially be the last	
	Brexitcast (.) before the summer holidays (.) but I am around (.) so you	
	might be hearing from me so anyway (.) here is the non-klaxon (.) normal	10
	Thursday (.) Brexitcast [jingle and intro slogan] I think we should start with	
	me (.) extending a bit of an olive branch to the newly re-appointed Brexit	
	secretary (.) Steve Barclay (1) do you remember the quiz?	
LK	I remember the quiz	15
AF	How could we ever forget (h.h.h.) I think he's probably trying to forget (.)	
	so I've now done the very very difficult quiz on a lot of people (.) including	
	people who actually (.) wrote parts of the Withdrawal Agreement	
LK	Do you mean the Keir Starmer Memorial Withdrawal Agreement Quiz?	
AF	No (.) this is the Steve Barclay Testimonial st. Withdrawal Agreement Quiz	20
LK	It's been	
AF	Steve Barclay Testimonial	
LK	Upgraded	
AF	When he got one and a half out of five	
LK	Yeh Oh God	25
AF	I've done it with (.) ten people now (.) only one person got more than (.)	
	Steve Barclay	
	[laughter]	
AF	so he's actually (.) at number two on the leader board	30
LK	This is big news for	
	the new Brexit secretary	
AF	So (.) you can stay Steve [laughter]	
LK	Well now Adam has approved the appointment of the new Brexit secretary	
	we can all say where we are (.) so it's Laura in Westminster with alongside	35
	me (.)	
CF	Caroline Flint	
AF	And Adam in Brussels	
LK	I'm happy to report Caroline has brought a huge box of doughnuts	
	[laughter]	40
LK	Which is splendid work (.) we ha we were however	
CF	I made them as well	
LK	Did you?	
CF	No [laughter]	
AF	I heard they might be mass produced	45
	[laughter]	
CF	I brought them with my own fair hands	
LK	Well I have to say that your team very kindly said Caroline would love to	
	come on Brexitcast (.) and she makes a good lemon drizzle	50
CF	I do (.) actually (.) I do (.) you know my kitchen is in Doncaster really	
LK	hmm	

CF   I did only have twenty minutes' notice of (.) arriving here so I'm afraid a
       certain popular (.) store that does pasties as well [laughter] provided these
       from Westminster station   55
LK   Very good (.) well I'm going to have one while em while while Adam
AK   Caroline (.) can I just ask you
LK   Yeh I'm going to have a doughnut
AF   Do you
CF   You ask your question   60
AF   In the in the nomenclature of Brexit (.) tribes (.) leavers (.) remainers (.)
       hard Brexit and all that
CF   Yeh
AF   How do we describe you

---

which is a pun based on the standard automated email response that is set at such times and the 'Office of State' of government.

If we look at the opening of this episode (Table 6.2), we can see the lack of temporal or spatial certainty means there is no 'good evening' or similarly clock-bound greeting. Instead, Fleming starts with the now semi-formal generic greeting of 'Hello' before evoking a sense of shared ownership of the broadcast by referring to listeners as 'Brexitcasters'. There is explicit mention of the time of recording ('Thursday late afternoon' lines 2–3), but also mention of this being the third such podcast of the week (prefaced as 'the non-klaxon' podcast in reference to the use of the klaxon for non-routine episodes). The reason is left unstated, although the arrival of Boris Johnson as new prime minister would have been the cause of the previous additional two podcasts for that particular week, elliptically referenced as a 'far from normal or chilled out' week (line 4). This use of colloquial language – 'chilled out' – is typical of the tone of this podcast. We have a description of the whereabouts of the absent journalists for this particular recording, again signposted as common knowledge ('as you know' line 6), and the four journalists are only listed by their first names, not as is in formal convention by their full names. We also see the production of an elaboration on Katya Adler's absence, with details of her family holiday and an expression of sympathy for the long car journey with young children (lines 6–7). All of this personal information enhances the sense of an intimate community of journalists and listeners.

The podcast assumes a substantial amount of shared knowledge with the listeners. A common experience of political turmoil underpins Fleming's joking conceit that the podcast could be the last one before the autumn, since Parliament is on its summer break. The understated reassurance that 'but I am around' (line 9) draws upon the shared understanding that a turbulent political summer is ahead and a number of remarkable events are likely. As well interpellating the audience as knowing participants in the conversation, this foregrounds the individual commitment and agency of the speaker and humorously conflates likely political events with the personal whim of the journalist.

This is all before the usual introductory jingle that is made up of soundbites that add light-hearted humour to the show (featuring quotations such as 'I think we could say that this is a dog's Brexit').

It is only after the jingle that we learn of the other journalist who is taking part in this podcast: Laura Kuenssberg. She is invited into the conversational floor space by a question posed by Fleming (line 13). This question – 'Do you remember the quiz?' – is also aimed at the listeners, and Kuenssberg's response confirms the memorability of the quiz that implicitly involves Barclay using mild taboo 'Oh god' (line 24). Fleming reminds the listeners that Brexit Secretary Steve Barclay had performed poorly in a Brexit quiz, describing it as 'the very very difficult quiz' (line 16), which carries the informality and ironic overstatement that comes from the double intensifier. This is then rendered more comedic within the shared political lexicon of the podcast community, by Kuenssberg's renaming it after the opposing Labour party's shadow Brexit secretary, Keir Starmer, before Fleming changes this to the name of hapless Steve Barclay (line 21).

This ridicule attached to this exchange on naming is contextualized by Fleming's assertion that some of the people who failed in the quiz included those who had been party the withdrawal agreement upon which the questions are based. The disproportionately high number of poor scores leads to Fleming's sardonic suggestion Barclay ranks high in a very poor field of entrants and 'you can stay Steve' (line 33). Both Fleming and Kuenssberg produce audible laughter at this remark, followed by Fleming's declaration that Barclay 'can stay' (line 31). Kuenssberg makes light of the obvious lack of authority Fleming has in this respect (the felicity conditions do not hold out) in her statement that 'Adam has approved the appointment of the new Brexit secretary' (line 32). This light-hearted bantering between the two journalists sets up the podcast to be less formal than the political interview programmes found in TV and radio broadcasts.

When Kuenssberg finally introduces the guest on line 34, this is framed around Flint having brought a box of doughnuts into the studio with her. There follows a light-hearted interaction on the subject of whether or not Flint made the doughnuts herself, including Fleming who is not in the studio with them. The norms of broadcast discussion are breached still further, with laughter and talking over one another, broken by phatic utterances such as Kuenssberg's announcement that she is 'going to have a doughnut' (line 55). We can see a great deal of overlap (lines 49, 60) and interruptions (e.g. 20–30). Thus, we can see that there is an informal atmosphere with journalists and interviewees all working together to retain a sense of light-hearted discussion, but within a settled arrangement of shared political knowledge.

As we can see (Table 6.3), although this podcast only features two of the usual four journalists, what is noticeable is that both of them are taking part at the same time: this is not a conventional news interview where one journalist will take the interviewer role. Instead, it is more of a conversation without the usual broadcast convention of news interviews having pre-allocated turn-taking:

Table 6.3

AF	In the in the nomenclature of Brexit (.) tribes (.) leavers (.) remainers (.) hard Brexit and all that	1
CF	Yeh	
AF	How do we describe you	
CF	Ooh em em em em er er I don't know (.) what am I what I am I a a Lexiter now I don't know in all this (.) I campaigned for Remain I voted for Remain (.) but once the result was through I just wanted us to get a deal and move on (.) and that's been my position since twenty sixteen pretty much	5
AF	And how does that compare with official Labour party policy?	10

CF   Well I I I sort of feel that I'm I've kept faith with what I thought was
      [laughter] official Labour party policy cos it's you know (.) what was that
      line on the first leaflet in the General Election twenty seventeen (.) er the
      the matter of leaving the European Union has been set by the British   15
      people erm er we will work to get the best deal erm but we're leaving (.)
      that's basically what we said and em that's what I've stuck with (.) I mean
      (h.) there are variations on this and I em I think it's one of those things like
      you know when people make speeches (.) and you can have a load of
      people in a room (.) and then then you basically poll those people off and   20
      say what did that person just say (.) and you come up with six different
      versions (.) you you know you sort of realise that after this sort of game
      that you know people just tend to hear that bit what they want to hear
AF   Mmm
CF   And so I think people are still taking what they can (.) as far as I can work 25
      out (.) Adam (.) we are still saying that if (.) by some chance (.) er (.) we
      haven't left the union left the European Union and we would form a
      government we would we would work for a Brexit deal (.) I think that's still
      in the pipeline (.) isn't it?
                                                                                   30
LK   Well I think so [CF laughter] but em it's a bit of as I tuck into my doughnut
      (.) it's a bit em like having your cake and eating it (.) isn't it (.) the Labour
      policy (.) so as I understand it (.) and it's fascinating that your interpretation
      of it is basically (.) you are still trying to do a Brexit deal
CF   Mmm
                                                                                   35
LK   Is that you would have to have a referendum on a Tory deal (.) or on a no
      deal (.) to try and stop someone else's version but your own version might
      be okay
CF   Yeh exactly (.) and if we like our version (.) why would we have a second
      referendum on it and why would we campaign for remain   40
LK   Yeh
CF   so it is very complicated isn't it and em as I say I try to keep track [laughter]
AF   No no you wouldn't be having a referendum on your own
      [laughter]
                                                                                   45
AF   deal
CF   No no
AF   You only have a referendum on the Tory deal
CF   Yeh (.) yeh (.) so basically (.) I think maybe some of my colleagues may be
      hoping that and who knows in in the scheme of things (.) I've been wrong
      about so many things over the past year in particular about what might   50
      happen we wouldn't have European Elections (.) we couldn't be mad
      enough but anyway (.)
AF   You you
CF   Maybe maybe our people are just hoping (.) despite everything they say (.)
      that a deal gets across the line then (.) maybe we can go back to having   55
      some semblance of possibly having a general election on other issues apart
      from Brexit

While important, the shift towards the informal and overlapping practices of conversation is not the full story, as we can see in the second part of this transcription. As the podcast continues, we can see that there is less overlapping talk and more uninterrupted stretches of speech with only conventional back channelling (lines 3, 22, 33). It is at this part of the podcast where the Labour politician interviewee is invited to speak in response to Fleming's question about what 'nomenclature' from the Brexit lexicon she would choose for herself. There is no challenge, even when she stumbles over her own explanation of Labour's policy on Brexit (lines 10–28), where she offers the potentially damaging concession that she is uncertain what party policy is. In the event, it is Flint herself who opts to bring her conversational turn to a conclusion (line 28) with a question directed to Fleming, where her tag is an outwardly earnest request for affirmation of her own party's policy ('isn't it?', line 27). Kuenssberg answers initially by emphasizing the informal style of the podcast by first directing the topic to her consumption of a doughnut, which is then developed into a metaphor ('Having your cake and eating it' – line 30). Only then does Kuenssberg turn to the complex position of the Labour Party, emphasizing its contradictions with the rhetorical repetition of 'version', and eliciting the agreement of Flint as to the accuracy of her account. All of this agreement of the misunderstanding and discord is ameliorated by shared laughter, and Flint is finally able to exit the discussion by asserting that Brexit has an undue prominence in political discussion (lines 51–54). In this way, we can see the interviewers regard this as an experiential interview (Montgomery, 2007) rather than the more traditional accountability interview featuring politicians.

We can see that there is an informal style that is characteristic of news podcasts, and that this is made light-hearted and even comedic by the journalists involved, as well as the interviewee. This exemplifies what Mia Lindgren (2016) describes as the 'personal narrative' component of the podcast, where the journalist displays their engagement with the form by revealing something of themselves. The opening of the podcast details the holiday plans of the absent journalists, and then there is a running trope of donut manufacture and consumption that recurs throughout. The participants cooperate in engaging in this informality, with the speakers overlapping and interrupting in a way that is not conventionally challenging or attentive to the opportunities for elaboration or probing associated with conventional political journalism. In discharging the priority of sustaining amusing conversation, this particular genre of political journalism has more in common with the chat show than those traditional accountability interviews we have seen in the first two chapters of this book.

Conclusion

What characterizes digital journalism is the rapidity of technological change. It is also apparent that the development of capacity and access to the means of news production are the causes of change within journalism culture itself. There are ever-greater opportunities for a more immediate relationship with unfolding events, which in turn require a more complex and nuanced relationship with the truth of interpretation. Importantly, the discourses that emerge need to remains true to those commitments to accuracy that should drive journalism of every form and on each media platform. Added to and integrated with this, we have seen the introduction of a raft of non-professional actors into journalism, both in the form of citizen journalists and the participants and bystanders that gather around a news event.

So where should our emphasis lie in analysing digital journalism? Such an analysis needs to set apart what distinguishes digital journalism from other forms, while appreciating where older discursive conventions remain in place. In this chapter, we have seen that many online news stories share the expressive and structural qualities of longer-established news platforms. But we have also explored the capacity of online news not only to update the news on a continual basis, but to do this cumulatively: that is, to display those updates as a progress towards journalistic understanding. The shifting relationship with the here-and-now of the news text has implications for the experience of reading the news. More importantly, for our purposes, the strategic use of tense, the ambivalence of unverified sourcing and the submission to a default tone of contingency have implications for the way journalism is composed. What we have seen, particularly in our discussion of podcasts, is that there is a clear shift towards informalization of news. The conversational style of the podcast has been adopted as a convention by professional journalists, and as such it is another marker of the increased informalization but also the socialization of news journalism.

Bibliography

Abu-Lughod, Lila (1990) 'The romance of resistance: tracing transformations of power through Bedouin women's lives', *American Ethnologist* 17: 41–55.

Allan, Stuart (2010) *News Culture* (3rd edition). Maidenhead: Open University Press.

Althusser, Louis (1971) *Lenin and Philosophy and Other Essays*. London: New Left Books.

Anderson, Benedict (2006) *Imagined Communities* (new edition). London: Verso.

Bakhtin, Mikhail M. (1986) *Speech Genres and Other Late Essays*. Austin: Texas University Press.

Baresch, Brian, Shih-Hsein Hsu and Stephen D. Reese (2012) 'The power of framing: new challenges for researching the structure of meaning in news', in Stuart Allan (ed.) *The Routledge Companion to News and Journalism* (revised edition). London: Routledge, pp. 637–47.

Barthes, Roland (1970/1975) *S/Z* (trans R. Miller). London: Cape.

Baxter, Judith (2014) *Double-Voicing at Work: Power, Gender and Linguistic Expertise*. Basingstoke: Palgrave.

BBC News (2011a) 'As it happened: Libya's Col Gaddafi killed'. http://www.bbc.co.uk/news/world-africa-15387872.

Beard, Adrian (1998) *The Language of Sport*. London: Routledge.

Bell, Allan (1991) *The Language of News*. Oxford: Blackwell.

Bell, Allan (1995) 'News time', *Time & Society* 4(3): 305–28.

Bell Allan (1999) 'News stories as narrative', in Adam Jaworski and Nicholas Coupland (eds) *The Discourse Reader*. London: Routledge, pp.236–51.

Bell, Alan and Peter Garrett (eds) (1998) *Approaches to Media Discourse*. Oxford: Blackwell.

Bennett, David (1998) (ed.) *Multicultural States: Rethinking Difference and Identity*. London: Routledge.

Benwell B. (ed.) (2003) *Masculinity and Men's Lifestyle Magazines*. Oxford: Blackwell.

Berners-Lee, Tim (2000) *Weaving the Web*. London: Texere.

Betz, Michelle (2018) 'Media noise and the complexity of conflicts: making sense of media in conflict prevention', Background Paper for the United Nations World Bank Flagship Study, *Pathways for Peace: Inclusive Approaches to Preventing Violent Conflict*. New York: World Bank.

Billig, Michael (1995) *Banal Nationalism*. London: Sage.

Bishop, Hywel and Adam Jaworski (2003) '"We beat 'em": nationalism and the hegemony of homogeneity in the British press reportage of Germany versus England during Euro 2000.' *Discourse and Society* 14(3): 234–71.

Blain, Neil and Hugh O'Donnell (1998) 'European sports journalism and its readers during Euro 96: living without *The Sun*' in M. Roche (ed.) *Sports, Popular Culture and Identity*. Aachen: Mayer and Mayer, pp 37–56.

Blake, James (2017) *Television and the Second Screen: Interactive TV in the Age of Social Participation*. Abingdon: Routledge.

Block, Mary Angela (2012) 'Citizen video journalists and authority in narrative: reviving the role of the witness', *Journalism: Theory, Practice and Criticism* 13(5): 639–53.

Bonner, Frances (2003) *Ordinary Television*. London: Sage

Bromley, Michael (2010) '"All the world's a stage": 24/7 news, newspapers and the ages of media', in Stephen Cushion and Justin Lewis (eds) *The Rise of 24-Hour News Television*. New York: Peter Lang, pp. 31–49.

Brookes, Rod, Justin Lewis and Karin Wahl-Jorgensen (2004) 'The media representation of public opinion: British television news coverage of the 2001 general election', *Media, Culture & Society* 26(1): 63–80.

Brown, Deirdre and Stephen Levinson (1987) *Politeness: Some Universals in Language Use*. Cambridge: Cambridge University Press.

Brown, R. and A. Gilman (1960) 'The pronouns of power and solidarity', in T.A. Sebeok (ed.) *Style in Language*. Cambridge, MA: MIT Press, pp. 253–76.

Bruns, Axel and Jean Burgess (2015) 'Twitter hashtags from ad hoc to calculated publics', in Nathan Rambukkana (ed.) *#Hashtag Publics: The Power and Politics of Discursive Networks*. New York: Peter Lang, pp. 13–27.

Brunsdon, Charlotte and David Morley (1978) *Everyday Television: 'Nationwide'*. London: BFI.

Burns, Lynette Sheridan and Benjamin J. Matthews (2018) *Understanding Journalism*. Thousand Oaks, CA: Sage.

Butler, J. (1990) Gender Trouble: Feminism and the Subversion of Identity. London: Routledge.

Cameron, Deborah (1990) *The Feminist Critique of Language*. London: Routledge.

Cameron, Deborah (2001) *Working with Spoken Discourse*. London: Sage.

Cameron, Deborah (ed.) (2006) *The Language and Sexuality Reader*. London: Routledge.

Carter, Ronald et al. (1997) *Working with Texts*. London: Routledge.

Chouliaraki, Lilie (2012) 'Journalism and the visual politics of war and conflict', in Stuart Allan (ed.) *The Routledge Companion to News and Journalism* (2nd edition). Abingdon: Routledge, pp. 520–33.

Chovanec, Jan. 2009. "'Call Doc Singh!" Textual structure and coherence in live text sports commentaries', in Olga Dontcheva-Navratilova and Renata Povolna (eds) *Coherence and Cohesion in Spoken and Written Discourse*. Newcastle upon Tyne: Cambridge Scholars Publishing, pp. 124–37.

Clayman, Stephen (1988) 'Displaying neutrality in television news interviews'. *Social Problems*, 35: 474–92

Clayman, Stephen (1992) 'Footing in the achievement of neutrality: the case of news interview discourse' in P. Drew and J. Heritage (eds) *Talk at Work*. Cambridge: Cambridge University Press, pp. 163–98.

Clayman, Stephen (2002) 'Tribune of the people: maintaining the legitimacy of aggressive journalism', *Media, Culture & Society* 24: 197–216.

Coates, Jennifer (1995) 'Language, gender and career', in Sara Mills (ed.) *Language and Gender: Interdisciplinary Perspectives*. London: Longman, pp. 13–30.

Coates, Jennifer (1996) *Women Talk: Conversation between Women Friends*. Oxford: Blackwell.

Conboy, Martin (2006) *Tabloid Britain: Constructing a Community through Language*. Abingdon: Oxford.

Connell, Robert W. (1987) *Gender and Power: Society, the Person and Sexual Politics*. Cambridge: Polity.

Corbett, James (2010) *England Expects: A History of the England Football Team* (revised edition). London: De Coubertin.

Crisell, Andrew (2012) *Liveness & Recording in the Media*. Basingstoke: Palgrave.

Cronin, Mike and David Mayall (eds) (1998) *Sporting Nationalisms: Identity, Ethnicity, Immigration and Assimilation*. London: Frank Cass.

Crystal, David (2010) 'Language developments in British English', in Michael Higgins, Clarissa Smith and John Storey (eds) *The Cambridge Companion to Modern British Culture*. Cambridge: Cambridge University Press, pp. 26–41.

Cushion, Stephen and Justin Lewis (eds) (2010) *The Rise of 24-Hour News Television*. New York: Peter Lang.

Davis, Anthony (1995) *Magazine Journalism Today*. Oxford: Focal Press.

Dayan, Daniel and Elihu (1992) *Media Events: The Live Broadcasting of History*. Cambridge, MA: Harvard University Press.

Delin, Judy (2000) *The Language of Everyday Life*. London: Sage.

Eagleton, Terry (1991) *Ideology: An Introduction*. London: Verso.

Edge, Abigail (2015) 'Mail Online almost at 200m monthly visitors in December'. *Journalism.com*, 22 January 2015. https://www.journalism.co.uk/news/abc-mail-online-on-verge-of-reaching-200-million-monthly-visitors-in-december/s2/a563873/(accessed 22 August 2019).

Elster, Jon (1982) 'Belief, bias and ideology', in Martin Hollis and Steven Lukes (eds) *Rationality and Relativism*. Oxford: Basil Blackwell, pp. 123–48.

Eriksson, Göran, Leoner Camauër and Yuliya Lakew (2017) 'Ordinary people on television: a longitudinal study of Swedish television 1982–2011', *Nordicom Review* 38 (2): 113–29.

Evan, Harold (1972) *Newsman's English*. London: Heinemann.

Fairclough, Norman (2001, 1st edition 1989) *Language and power*. Harlow: Longman.

Fairclough, Norman (1992) *Discourse and Social Change*. London: Sage.

Fairclough, Norman (1993) 'Critical Discourse Analysis and the marketization of public discourse: the universities', *Discourse and Society* 2: 133–68.

Fairclough, Norman (1995a) *Critical Discourse Analysis: The Critical Study of Language*. Harlow: Longman.

Fairclough, Norman (1995b) *Media Discourse*. London: Arnold.

Fairclough, Norman (1998) 'Political discourse in the media: an analytical approach', in Alan Bell and Peter Garrett (eds) *Approaches to Media Discourse*. Oxford: Blackwell, pp. 142–62.

Fairclough, Norman (2001) 'Critical discourse analysis as a method in social scientific research', in Ruth Wodak and Michael Meyer (eds) *Methods of Critical Discourse Analysis*. London: Sage, pp. 121–38.

Fairclough, Norman (2003) *Analysing Discourse: Textual Analysis for Social Research*. London: Routledge.

Fairclough, Norman and Ruth Wodak (1997) 'Critical discourse analysis', in T.A. van Dijk (ed.) *Discourse as Social Interaction*. London: Sage, pp. 258–84.

Fenton, Natalie (2012) 'News in the digital age', in Stuart Allan (ed.) *The Routledge Companion to News and Journalism* (revised edition). Abingdon: Routledge, pp. 557–67.

Foucault, Michel (1970) 'Orders of discourse', *Social Science Information* 10(2): 7–30.

Foucault, Michel (1980) *Power/Knowledge: Selected Interviews and Other Writings 1972–1977*. Hemel Hempstead: Harvester Wheatsheaf.

Foucault, Michel (1981) 'The Order of discourse', in R. Young (ed.) *Untying the Text: A Poststructuralist Reader*. Oxford: Basil Blackwell, pp. 48–78.

Foucault, Michel (1983) 'The subject and power', in Hubert L. Dreyfus and Paul Rabinow (eds) *Michel Foucault: Beyond Structuralism and Hermeneutics* (2nd edition). Chicago, IL: Chicago University Press, pp. 208–26.

Fowler, Roger, Bob Hodge, Gunther Kress and Tony Trew (1979) *Language and Control*. London: Routledge.

Frow, John (1989) 'Discourse and power', in Mike Gane (ed.) *Ideological Representation and Power in Social Relations*. London: Routledge, pp. 198–217.

Galtung, Johan and Mari Ruge (1965) 'The structure of foreign news. The presentation of the Congo, Cuba and Cyprus crises in four Norwegian newspapers', *Journal of Peace Research* 2: 64–90.

Garland, J. and M. Rowe (1999) 'Selling the game short: an examination of the role of antiracism in British football', *Socioloigy of Sport Journal* 16(1): 35–53.

Gauntlett, David (2002) *Media, Gender and Identity*. London: Routledge.

Gee, Paul (1999) *An Introduction to Discourse Analysis: Theory and Method*. London: Routledge.

Gellner, Ernest (1983) *Nations and Nationalism*. Oxford: Blackwell.

Glaser, Mark (2012) 'Citizen journalism: widening world views, extending democracy', in Stuart Allan (ed.) *The Routledge Companion to News and Journalism* (revised edition). Abingdon: Routledge, pp. 578–90.

Goddard, Angela (1998) *The Language of Advertising*. London: Routledge.

Goffman, Erving (1959) *The Presentation of Self in Everyday Life*. Harmondsworth: Penguin.

Goffman, E. (1981) *Forms of Talk*. Oxford: Blackwell.

Goggin, Gerard (2013) 'Sport and the rise of mobile media', in David Rowe and Brett Hutchins (eds) *Media Sport: Technology, Power and Identity in Network Society*. New York: Routledge, pp. 1–15.

Graddol, David, Jenny Chesire and Joan Swann (1999 (1994)) *Describing Language*. Buckingham: Open University Press.

Gramsci, Antonio (1971) *Selections from the Prison Notebooks*. London: Lawrence & Wishart.

Gramsci, Antonio (1998) *Prison Letters* (trans Hamish Henderson). London: Pluto Press.

Grice, H. Paul (1975) 'Logic and conversation', in Peter Cole and Jerry L. Morgan (eds) *Syntax and Semantics 3: Speech Acts*. New York: Academic Press, pp. 41–58.

Habermas, Jurgen (1987) *Theory of Communicative Action, Vol. 1*. London: Heinemann.

Hall, Stuart (1992) 'The question of cultural identity', in Stuart Hall, David Held and Anthony G. McGrew (eds) *Modernity and Its Futures*. Cambridge: Polity, pp. 273–325.

Hall, Stuart (1997) *Representation: Cultural Representations and Signifying Practices*. London: Sage.

Halliday, Michael A. K. (1975) 'Anti-languages', *American Anthropologist* 78(3): 570–84.

Harcup, Tony (2009) *Journalism: Principles and Practice* (2nd edition). London: Sage.

Harcup, Tony and Deirdre O'Neill (2001) 'What is news? Gatlung and Ruge revisited', *Journalism Studies* 2(2): 261–80.

Harcup, Tony and Deirdre O'Neill (2017) 'What is news? News values revisited (again)', *Journalism Studies* 18(12): 1470–88.

Hartley, John and Martin Montgomery (1985) 'Representation and relations: ideology and power in the press and TV news', in Van Dijk (ed.) *Discourse and Communication*. Berlin: Walter de Gruyter, pp. 233–69.

Helmer, James (1993) 'Storytelling in the creation and maintenance of organizational tension and stratification', *The Southern Communication Journal* 59: 34–44.

Hemmingway, Emma and Joos van Loon (2010) "We'll always stay with live until we have something better to go to …': the chronograms of 24-hour television news', *Time & Society* 20(2): 149–70.

Hennessy, Brendan (1989) *Writing Feature Articles: A Practical Guide to Methods and Markets*. Oxford: Heinemann.

Heritage, J. (1985) 'Analysing news interviews' in Teun van Dijk (ed.) *Handbook of Discourse Analysis, Vol 3: Discourse and Dialogue*. London: Academic Press, pp. 95–117.

Heritage, John and David Greatbatch (1991) 'On the institutional character of institutional talk: the case of news interviews', in Deirdre Boden and Don H. Zimmerman (eds) *Talk and Social Structures: Studies in Ethnomethodology and Conversation Analysis*. Cambridge: Polity Press, pp. 93–137.

Hermida, Alfred (2009) 'The blogging BBC', *Journalism Practice* 3(3): 268–84.

Higgins, M. (2004) 'Putting the nation in the news', *Discourse & Society* 15(5): 633–48.

Higgins, Michael (2006) 'Substantiating a political public sphere in the Scottish press', *Journalism: Theory, Practice and Criticism* 7(1): 25–44.

Higgins, M. (2008) *Media and Their Publics*. Maidenhead: Open University Press.

Higgins, Michael (2010) 'British newspapers today', in M. Higgins, C. Smith and J. Storey (eds) *The Cambridge Companion to Modern British Culture*. Cambridge: Cambridge University Press, pp. 279–95.

Higgins, Michael and Angela Smith (2011) 'Not one of U.S.: Kate Adie's report of the 1986 US bombing of Tripoli and its critical aftermath', *Journalism Studies* 12(3): 344–58.

Higgins, Michael and Angela Smith (2017) *Belligerent Broadcasting: Synthetic Argument in Broadcast Talk*. Abingdon: Routledge.

Hodge, Robert and Gunther Kress (1993, 1st edition 1979) *Language as Ideology*. London: Routledge.

Hodge, Robert and Gunther Kress (1993) *Language as Ideology* (2nd edition). Abingdon: Routledge.

Hobsbawn, Eric J. (1990) *Nations and Nationalism since 1780*. Cambridge: Cambridge University Press.

Hobsbawm, Eric J. and Terence Ranger (eds) (1983) *The Invention of Tradition*. Cambridge: Cambridge University Press.

Holquist, Michael (1981) *Dialogism: Bakhtin and His Works*. London: Routledge.

Hong, Sounman (2012) 'Online news on Twitter: newspapers' social media adoption and their online readership', *Information, Economics and Policy* 24: 69–74.

Horton, Donald and Richard R. Wohl (1982) 'Mass communication and para-social interaction: observation of intimacy at a distance', in Garry Gumpert and Robert Cathcart (eds) *Inter/Media: Interpersonal Communication in a Media World*. New York: Oxford University Press, pp. 185–206.

Hutchby, Ian (1996) *Confrontation Talk*. Mahwah, NJ: Lawrence Erlbaum Associates.

Hutchby, Ian (2006) *Media Talk*. Maidenhead: Open University Press.

Jackson, Peter, Nick Stevenson and Kate Brooks (2001) *Making Sense of Men's Magazines*. Cambridge: Polity.

Johnson, Sammye and Patricia Prijatel (1999) *The Magazine: From Cover to Cover. Inside a Dynamic Industry*. New York: NTC Publishing.

Kress, Gunther (1985) *Linguistic Process in Sociocultural Practice*. Geelong, Victoria: Deakin University Press.

Kress, Gunther and Terry Threadgold (1988) 'Towards a social theory of genre', *Southern Review* 21(3): 215–43.

Kress, Gunther and Theo van Leeuwen (2001) *Multi-Modal Discourse: The Modes and Media of Contemporary Communication*. London: Arnold.

Kroon, Åsa (2017) 'More than a hashtag: producers' and users' co-creation of a loving "we" in Second Screen TV production', *Television and New Media* 18(7): 670–88.

Kroon Lundell, Åsa (2014) 'Cross-platform television: superliveness, metadiscourse and complex audience orientation in a sports journalism production on the web', *Northern Lights* 12: 11–27.

Kuiper, Koenraad (1995) *Smooth Talkers: The Linguistic Performance of Auctioneers and Sportscasters*. New York: Routledge.

Kuiper, Koenraad and Robyn Lewis (2013) 'The effect of the broadcast medium on the language of radio and television sports commentary genres: The rugby union lineout', *Journal of Sports Media* 8(2): 31–51.

Kunert, Jessica and Neil Thurman (2019) 'The form of content personalisation at mainstream, transatlantic news organisations: 2010–2016', *Journalism Practice* 13(7): 759–80.

Labov, William (1972) *Sociolinguistic Patterns*. Philadelphia: University of Pennsylvania Press.

Labov, William and J. Walestsky (1967) 'Narrative analysis: oral versions of personal experience', in J. Helm (ed.) *Essays on the Verbal and Visual Arts*. Seattle: University of Washington Press, pp. 12–44.

Lewis, Justin et al. (ud) *Too Close for Comfort? The Role of Embedded Reporting during the 2003 Iraq War: Summary report*. Cardiff: JOMEC.

Lindgren, Mia (2016) 'Personal narrative journalism and podcasting', *Radio Journal: International Studies in Broadcast & Audio Media* 14(1): 23–41.

Love, Ruth Leeds (1965) 'The business of television the black weekend', in Bradley S. Greenberg and Edwin B. Parker (eds) *The Kennedy Assassination and the American Public*. Stanford: Stanford University Press, pp. 73–86.

McCombs, Maxwell (2004) *Setting the Agenda: The Mass Media and Public Opinion*. Cambridge: Polity.

McCracken, Ellen (1992) *Decoding Women's Magazines*. Basingstoke: Macmillan.

Macdonald, Myra (1995) *Representing Women: Myths of Femininity in the Popular Media*. London: Arnold.

Macdonald, Myra (2003) *Exploring Media Discourse*. London: Arnold.

Maguire, Joseph (1999) and Jason Tuck (1998) 'Global sports and patriot games: rugby union and national identity in the United Sporting Kingdom since 1945', in Mike Cronin and David Mayall (eds) *Sporting Nationalisms*. London: Frank Cass, pp. 103–26.

Maguire, Joseph (1999) Emma Poulton and Catherine Possamai 'Weltkrieg III? Media coverage of England versus German in Euro 96', *Journal of Sport and Social Issues* 23(4): 439–54.

Marriott, Stephanie (2007) *Live Television*. London: Sage.

Marshall, Jill and Werndly Angela (2002) *The Language of Television*. London: Routledge.

Matheson, Donald (2005) *Media Discourses: Analysing Media Texts*. Maidenhead: Open University Press.

McCracken, Ellen (1993) *Decoding Women's Magazines*. Basingstoke: Macmillan.

McLoughlin, Linda (2000) *The Language of Magazines*. London: Routledge.

Miller, Casey and Kate Swift (1995) *The Handbook of Non-sexist Writing for Writers*. London: Women's Press.

Montgomery, Martin (1995) *An Introduction to Language and Society*. London: Routledge.

Montgomery, Martin (2006) 'Broadcast news, the live 'two-way' and the case of Andrew Gilligan', *Media, Culture and Society* 28(2): 233–59.

Montgomery, Martin (2007) *The Discourse of Broadcast News: A Linguistic Approach*. London: Routledge.

Montgomery, Martin (2019) *Language, Media and Culture: The Key Concepts*. London: Routledge.

Montgomery, Martin, Michael Higgins and Angela Smith (2019) 'Political offensiveness in the mediated public sphere: the performative play of alignments', in Ann Graefer (ed.) *Media and the Politics of Offence*, Basingstoke: Palgrave, pp. 23–46.

Morley, David (1980) *The 'Nationwide' Audience*. London: BFI.

Mouffe, Chantal (2005) *On the Political*. London: Routledge.

Myers, Greg (1994) *Words in Ads*. London: Arnold.

Nah, Shungahn and Deborah S. Chung (2012) 'When citizens meet both professional and citizen journalists: social trust, media credibility, and perceived journalistic roles among online community news readers', *Journalism: Theory, Practice and Criticism* 13(6): 714–30.

O'Donnell, Hugh (1994) 'Mapping the mythical: a geopolitics of national sporting stereotypes', *Discourse & Society* 5(3): 345–80.

Ofcom (2011) *The Ofcom Broadcasting Code*. London: Ofcom.

Ofcom (2017) *The Ofcom Broadcasting Code*. London: Ofcom.

Pearce, Michael (2006) *The Routledge Dictionary of English Language Studies*. London: Routledge.

Peters, John Durham (2001) 'Witnessing', *Media, Culture & Society* 23(6): 707–23

Phillips, Angela (2012) 'Sociability, speed and quality in the changing news environment', *Journalism Practice* 6(5–6): 669–79.

Quirk, Randolph, Sydney Greenbaum, Geoffrey Leech and Jan Svartvik (1985) *A Comprehensive Grammar of the English Language*. London: Longman.

Rambukkana, Nathan (2015) '#Introduction: hashtags as technosocial events', in Nathan Rambukkana (ed.) *#Hashtag Publics: The Power and Politics of Discursive Networks*. New York: Peter Lang, pp. 1–10.

Reah, Danuta (1998) *The Language of Newspapers*. London: Routledge.

Reisigl, Martin and Ruth Wodak (2001) *Discourses of Discrimination: Rhetorics of Racism and Anti-Semitism*. London: Routledge.

Roberts, Ian (2004) 'Saddam Hussein's medical examination should not have been broadcast: images were designed to humiliate', *British Medical Journal* 328(7430): 51.

Rowe, David (2004) *Sport, Culture and the Media* (2nd edition). Maidenhead: Open University Press.

Rowe, David (2007) 'Sports journalism: still the "toy department" of the news media?', *Journalism: Theory, Practice and Criticism* 8(4): 385–405.

Rusbridger, Alan (2018) *Breaking News*. Edinburgh: Canongate.

Saarkoski, Saska (2012) *Brands, Stars and Regular Hacks*. Oxford: Reuters Institute for the Study of Journalism.

Sacks, Harvey (1992) *Lectures in Conversation*. Oxford: Blackwell.

Sacks, Harvey, Emanuel A. Schegloff and Gail Jefferson (1974) 'A simplest systematics for the organisation of turn-taking for conversation', *Language* 50(4), part 1 (December 1974): 696–735.

Scannell, Paddy (ed.) (1991) 'Introduction: the relevance of talk', in Scannell (ed.) Broadcast Talk, London: Sage, pp. 1–13.

Scannell, Paddy (1996) *Radio, Television and Modern Life*. Oxford: Blackwell.

Schiffrin, Deborah (1984) 'Jewish argument as sociability', *Language in Society* 13(3): 311–35.

Schneider, Tanja and Teresa Davis (2010) 'Fostering a hunger for health: food and the self in "The Australian Women's Weekly"', *Healthy Sociology Review* 19(3): 285–303.

Schudson, Michael (1982) 'The ideal of conversation in the study of mass media', in Gary Gumpert and Robert Cathcart (eds) *Inter/Media: Interpersonal Communication in a Media World*, New York: Oxford University Press, pp. 41–8.

Schudson, Michael (2001) 'The objectivity norm in American journalism', *Journalism* 2(2): 149–70.

Seargeant, Philip (2019) *The Emoji Revolution: How Technology Is Shaping the Future of Communication*. Cambridge: Cambridge University Press.

Searle, John R. (1969) *Speech Acts: An Essay on the Philosophy of Language*. Cambridge: Cambridge University Press.

Senden, M. G., Back, E. A. and Lindqvist, A. (2015) 'Introducing a Gender Neutral Pronoun in a Natural Gender Language: The Influence of Time on Attitudes and Behaviour', Frontiers in Psychology, 6, doi: 10.3389/fpsyg.2015.00893/full.

Silberstein, Sandra (2002) *War of Words: Language, Politics and 9/11*. London: Routledge.

Simpson, Paul (1993) *Language, Ideology and Point of View*. London: Routledge.

Smith, Angela (2009) 'Tabloid television', in Christopher H. Sterling (ed.) *Encyclopaedia of Journalism* 4: Q-Z. Thousand Oaks, CA: Sage, pp. 1365–68.

Smith, Angela and Michael Higgins (2012) 'The convenient ambiguity of tone', *Journalism: Theory, Practice and Criticism* 13(8): 1081–95.

Smith, Anthony D. (1991) *National Identity*. Harmondsworth: Penguin.

Smith, Anthony D. (1998) *Nationalism and Modernism*. London: Routledge.

Spender, Dale (1980) *Man Made Language*. London: Routledge.

Sperber, Dan and Deirdre Wilson (1995) *Relevance: Communication and Cognition*. 2nd edition. Oxford: Blackwell.

Spiegl, Fritz (1989) *Mediawrite/Mediaspeak*. London: Elm Tree.

Starkey, Guy (2007) *Balance and Bias in Journalism*. London: Routledge.

Storey, John (1997) *An Introduction to Cultural Theory and Popular Culture*. Hemel Hempstead: Harvester Wheatsheaf.

Talbot, Mary (1995) 'A synthetic sisterhood: false friends in a teenage magazine', in Kira Hall and Mary Bucholtz (eds) *Gender Articulated: Language and the Socially Constructed Self*. London: Routledge, pp. 143–65.

Talbot, Mary (2010, first edition 1998) *Language and Gender (Second edition)*. Cambridge: Polity.

Talbot, Mary, Karen Atkinson and David Atkinson (2003) *Language and Power in the Modern World*. Edinburgh: Edinburgh University Press.

Tannen, Deborah (1991) *You Just Don't Understand*. London: Virago.

Tannen, Deborah (1995) *Talking from 9 to 5*. London: Virago.

Temple, Mick (2008) *The British Press*. Maidenhead: Open University Press.

Thibault, Paul J. (1991) *Social Semiotics as Praxis: Text, Social Meaning Making, and Nabakov's Ada*. Minneapolis: University of Minnesota Press.

Thompson, John B. (1995) *The Media and Modernity*. Cambridge: Polity.

Thornborrow, Joanna (2015) *The Discourse of Public Participation Media: From Talk Show to Twitter*. Abingdon: Routledge.

Threadgold, Terry (1989) 'Talking about genre: ideologies and incompatible discourses', *Cultural Studies* 2(1): 101–27.

Threadgold, Terry (1997) *Feminist Poetics: Poiesis, Performance, Histories*. London: Routledge.

Thurman, Neil (2008) 'Forums for citizen journalists? Adoption of user generated content initiatives by online news media', *New Media and Society* 10(1): 139–57.

Thurnman, Neil (2011) 'Making "The Daily Me": technology, economics and habit in the mainstream assimilation of personalized news', *Journalism: Theory, Practice & Criticism* 12(4): 395–415.

Tolson, Andrew (2006) *Media Talk: Spoken Discourse on TV and Radio*. Edinburgh: Edinburgh University Press.

Tuchman, Gaye (1972) 'Objectivity as strategic ritual: an examination of newsmen's notions of objectivity', *American Journal of Sociology* 77(4): 660–79.

Tulloch, John and Colin Sparks (2000) *Tabloid Tales*. London: Rowman and Littlefield.\

Van Dijk, Teun (1983) *News as Discourse*. Hillsdale, NJ: LEA.

Van Dijk (1988) *News as Discourse*. Hillsdale, NJ: Lawrence Erlbaum.

Van Dijk, Teun (1991) *Racism and the Press*. London: Routledge.

Vesanen, Jan (2007) 'What is personalisation? A conceptual framework', *European Journal of Marketing* 41(5/6): 409–18.

Wahl-Jorgensen, Karen (2019) *Emotions, Media and Politics*. Cambridge: Polity.

Warad, Katie (2020) 'Understanding gender categorisation in a binary society' in Angela Smith (ed) Gender Equalityi n Changing Times. Bsingstoke: Palgrave.

Whannell, Gary (1992) *Fields of Vision: Television Sport and Cultural Transformation*. London: Routledge.

Williamson, Judith (1995) *Decoding Advertisements: Ideology and Meaning in Advertising*. London: Marion Boyers Publishing.

Wodak, Ruth (1996) *Disorders of Discourse*. Harlow: Longman.

Wodak, Ruth (2002) 'The discourse-historical approach', in Ruth Wodak and Michael Meyer (eds) (2002) *Methods of Critical Discourse Analysis*. London: Sage.

Wodak Ruth and Tuen van Dijk (2000) *Racism at the Top*. Klagenfurt: Drava.

Wodak, Ruth and J.R. Martin (eds) (2003) *Re/reading the Past: Critical and Functional Perspectives on Time and Value*. Amsterdam: John Benjamins, pp. 87–121.

Wodak, Ruth and Michael Meyer (2009) 'Critical discourse analysis: history, agenda, theory and methodology', in Ruth Wodak and Michael Meyer (eds) *Methods of Critical Discourse Analysis* (2nd edition). London: Sage, pp. 1–33.

Yule, George (1996) *Pragmatics*. Oxford: Oxford University Press.

Wodak, Ruth, Rudolf de Cellia, Martin Reisigl and Karin Liebhart (1999) *The Discursive Construction of National Identity*. Edinburgh: Edinburgh University Press.

Wodak, Ruth, Peter Nowak, Johanna Pelokan, Helmut Gruber, Rudolf de Cillia and Richard Mitten (1990) *Wir sind alle unschuldige Täter!: Diskurshistorische Studien zum Nachkriegsantisemitismus*. Frankfurt: Suhrkamp.

Index